NORTON CRITICAL SCORES

BACH   **CANTATA NO. 4**
edited by Gerhard Herz

BACH   **CANTATA NO. 140**
edited by Gerhard Herz

BEETHOVEN   **SYMPHONY NO. 5 IN C MINOR**
edited by Elliot Forbes

BERLIOZ   **FANTASTIC SYMPHONY**
edited by Edward T. Cone

CHOPIN   **PRELUDES, OPUS 28**
edited by Thomas Higgins

DEBUSSY   **PRELUDE TO "THE AFTERNOON OF A FAUN"**
edited by William W. Austin

HAYDN   **SYMPHONY NO. 103 IN E-FLAT MAJOR ("DRUM ROLL")**
edited by Karl Geiringer

MOZART   **PIANO CONCERTO IN C MAJOR, K. 503**
edited by Joseph Kerman

MOZART   **SYMPHONY IN G MINOR, K. 550**
edited by Nathan Broder

SCHUBERT   **SYMPHONY IN B MINOR ("UNFINISHED")**
edited by Martin Chusid

SCHUMANN   **DICHTERLIEBE**
edited by Arthur Komar

STRAVINSKY   **PETRUSHKA**
edited by Charles Hamm

WAGNER   **PRELUDE and TRANSFIGURATION from
TRISTAN AND ISOLDE**
edited by Robert Bailey

Ludwig van Beethoven

SYMPHONY NO. 5
IN C MINOR

An Authoritative Score · The Sketches
Historical Background
Analysis · Views and Comments

Edited by

ELLIOT FORBES

PROFESSOR EMERITUS, HARVARD UNIVERSITY

W · W · NORTON & COMPANY

New York · London

W. W. Norton & Company, Inc., 500 Fifth Avenue, New York, N.Y. 10110
W. W. Norton & Company Ltd., 37 Great Russell Street, London WC1B 3NU

Library of Congress Catalog Card No. 73-98890
PRINTED IN THE UNITED STATES OF AMERICA
9 0

ISBN 0-393-09893-1

Contents

Preface   *vi*

Historical Background   *3*

The Score of the Symphony

     1st Movement   Allegro con brio   *19*

     2nd Movement   Andante con moto   *38*

     3rd Movement   Allegro   *53*

     4th Movement   Allegro   *68*

     The Sketches   *117*

     Textual Note   *129*

Analysis

     Donald Francis Tovey · [The Fifth Symphony]   *143*

     E. T. A. Hoffmann · [Review of the Fifth Symphony]   *150*

     Heinrich Schenker · [The First Movement]   *164*

Views and Comments

     Anton Schindler   *185*

     Ludwig Spohr   *186*

     Hector Berlioz   *187*

     Felix Mendelssohn   *190*

     Richard Wagner   *191*

     Felix Weingartner   *194*

     Donald Francis Tovey   *198*

     Edward T. Cone   *199*

Bibliography   *201*

Preface

At the end of the last century, Sir George Grove in his book on *Beethoven and his Nine Symphonies* wrote of the Fifth Symphony, "We have now arrived at the piece of music by which Beethoven is most widely known." The same is probably true today. The rhythm of the first four notes became a symbol of resistance throughout Europe during the terror of the Second World War. Not only in England could it be said that "the C minor Symphony always fills the room."

The editor attempts to give a version of the orchestral score which conforms to Beethoven's original details as represented by his own autograph. I have drawn from Heinrich Schenker's reading of this autograph, and his own list of discrepancies between the autograph and the printed score has also been included.

The historical introduction is a biographical study of Beethoven's compositional activity from 1804 to 1808, the years in which the symphony developed from sketches to its final form. A discussion of the sketches follows, the first readily accessible survey of this material in English.

From among the many analyses of the work, I have chosen, first, Tovey's general treatment of the symphony as a whole. Then, the first serious review of this work, by E. T. A. Hoffmann, is given for the first time in English in its entirety. There follows Heinrich Schenker's analysis in depth of the first movement, also translated into English for the first time. Finally, there are views and comments on different aspects of this music by writers from Beethoven's time to our own.

The bibliography has been selected primarily from sources in English which shed light on Beethoven as a man, Beethoven as a writer of symphonies, or on specific problems concerning this particular symphony.

I would like to thank F. John Adams, Jr. for his help in the translations of the Hoffmann and Schenker texts; Professor Allen Forte for his assistance in clarifying certain points in the Schenker translation; and David Hamilton for his helpful suggestions and general guidance in the preparation of this edition.

Elliot Forbes

HISTORICAL
BACKGROUND

Historical Background

Approximately seven years after his move from Bonn to Vienna, Beethoven at the age of 29 years completed his first symphony. Characteristically, however, there are symphonic sketches dating back even to the Bonn period. One of the earliest sketches in C minor, marked "Sinfonia," is a prophecy, not only in its key but in its spirit, of the Fifth Symphony:[1]

1. *Ludwig van Beethoven. Autograph Miscellany from circa 1785 to 1799*, ed. Joseph Kerman, London, 1970, II, p. 175.

Beethoven had already used the theme in the first allegro section (in E♭ minor) of his first piano quartet, WoO 36,[2] written in 1785.

The First Symphony was first performed on April 2nd, 1800; and the momentum towards symphonic composition that it generated was not to slacken for eight years, by which time Beethoven had written six of his nine symphonies. The Second was completed in the fall of 1802 and the Third (*Eroica*) just a year later—an amazingly short period considering the compositional growth which this represents.

The next four years—specifically, from the spring of 1804 to the spring of 1808—form the period in which the Fifth Symphony took shape, a period of simultaneous creation of many masterpieces: the Sonatas, Opp. 53, 54 and 57; the Fourth Piano Concerto; the "Razumovsky" Quartets; the Fourth Symphony; the Violin Concerto; the first two versions of *Fidelio*; the Overture to *Coriolan*; the Mass in C; and the Cello Sonata in A major. And, as we shall see, this was followed during the year of 1808 by the composition of the Sixth Symphony, so that both symphonies (Nos. 5 and 6) could receive their first performances simultaneously before the end of the year. This period then deserves close study; here we will trace how Beethoven started to work on the Fifth, became sidetracked into completing the Fourth, resumed work on the Fifth and followed it immediately with the Sixth.

We may turn to Beethoven's friend Ignaz von Seyfried for a reliable description of the composer during this period:[3]

> Beethoven was much too straightforward, open and tolerant to give offense to another by disapprobation, or contradiction; he was wont to laugh heartily at what did not please him and I confidently believe that I may safely say that in all his life he never, at least not consciously, made an enemy; only those to whom his peculiarities were unknown were unable quite to understand how to get along with him; I am speaking here of an earlier time, before the misfortune of deafness had come upon him; if, on the contrary, Beethoven sometimes carried things to an extreme in his rude honesty in the case of many, mostly those who had imposed themselves upon him as protectors, the fault lay only in this, that the honest German always carried his heart on his tongue and understood everything better than how to flatter; also because, conscious of his own merit, he would never permit himself to be made the plaything of the vain whims of the Maecenases who were eager to boast of their association with the name and fame of the celebrated master. And so he was misunderstood

2. WoO = Werke ohne Opuszahl (Works without opus number). Cf. Georg Kinsky, *Das Werk Beethovens*, completed and edited by Hans Halm, Munich, 1955.
3. *Cäcilia*, Vol. IX, pp. 218–29, transl. A. W. Thayer. See *Thayer's Life of Beethoven*, ed. E. Forbes, Princeton, 1964, p. 370.

only by those who had not the patience to get acquainted with the apparent eccentric. When he composed "Fidelio," the oratorio "Christus am Ölberg," the symphonies in E-flat, C minor and F, the Pianoforte Concertos in C minor and G major, and the Violin Concerto in D, we were living in the same house and (since we were each carrying on a bachelor's apartment) we dined at the same restaurant and chatted away many an unforgettable hour in the confidential intimacy of colleagues, for Beethoven was then merry, ready for any jest, happy, full of life, witty and not seldom satirical.

Vienna first became aware of Beethoven's enormous talent, which from 1792 on was transforming her musical scene, through his displays of keyboard virtuosity both in public concerts and in the private houses of the aristocracy, many of whom became the composer's active patrons. But by 1804 Beethoven was no longer inclined to play his own music in public. According to his pupil, Ferdinand Ries[4]:

he wanted only to conduct and improvise. This last was certainly the most extraordinary [performance] any one was ever privileged to listen to, especially when he was in good humor or excited. Not a single artist of all that I have heard ever reached the plane in this respect which Beethoven occupied. The wealth of ideas which crowded in upon him, the moods to which he surrendered himself, the variety of treatment, the difficulties which offered themselves or were introduced by him, were inexhaustible.

Concerning his conducting we turn again to Seyfried:[5]

Our master could not be presented as a model in respect of conducting, and the orchestra always had to have a care in order not to be led astray by its mentor; for he had ears only for his composition and was ceaselessly occupied by manifold gesticulations to indicate the desired expression. He often made a down beat for an accent in the wrong place. He used to suggest a *diminuendo* by crouching down more and more, and at a *pianissimo* he would almost creep under the desk. When the volume of sound grew he rose up also as if out of a stage-trap, and with the entrance of the power of the band he would stand upon the tips of his toes almost as big as a giant, and waving his arms, seemed about to soar upwards to the skies. Everything about him was active, not a bit of his organism idle, and the man was comparable to a *perpetuum mobile*. He did not belong to those capricious composers whom no orchestra in the world can satisfy. At times, indeed, he was altogether too considerate and did not even repeat passages which went badly at the rehearsal: "It will go better next time," he would say. He was very particular about expression, the delicate nuances, the equable distribution of light and shade as well as an effective

4. *Biographische Notizen über Ludwig van Beethoven*, Coblenz, 1838, p. 99. See Thayer, op. cit., pp. 467–68.
5. *L. v. Beethovens Studien*, Appendix, transl. H. H. Pierson, Leipzig, 1853.

tempo rubato, and without betraying vexation, would discuss them with the individual players. When he then observed that the players would enter into his intentions and play together with increasing ardor, inspired by the magical power of his creations, his face would be transfigured with joy, all his features beamed pleasure and satisfaction, a pleased smile would play around his lips and a thundering "Bravi tutti!" reward the successful achievement. It was the first and loftiest triumphal moment for the genius, compared with which, as he confessed, the tempestuous applause of a receptive audience was as nothing. When playing at first sight, there were frequent pauses for the purpose of correcting the parts and then the thread would be broken; but he was patient even then; but when things went to pieces, particularly in the scherzos of his symphonies at a sudden and unexpected change of rhythm, he would shout with laughter and say he had expected nothing else, but was reckoning on it from the beginning; he was almost childishly glad that he had been successful in "unhorsing such excellent riders."

Beethoven's energies, however, were primarily spent in the sketching and shaping of a variety of works, most of which were great in scope. Seyfried describes the domestic scene with these words:[6]

He was never found on the street without a small note-book in which he was wont to record his passing ideas. Whenever conversation turned on the subject he would parody Joan of Arc's words: *"I dare not come without my banner!"*—and he adhered to his self-given rule with unparalleled tenacity; although otherwise a truly admirable disorder prevailed in his household. Books and music were scattered in every corner; here the remnants of a cold luncheon; here sealed or half-emptied bottles; here upon a stand the hurried sketches of a quartet; here the remains of a déjeuner; there on the pianoforte, on scribbled paper the material for a glorious symphony still slumbering in embryo; here a proof-sheet awaiting salvation; friendly and business letters covering the floor; between the windows a respectable loaf of strachino, *ad latus* a considerable ruin of a genuine Veronese salami—yet despite this varied mess our master had a habit, quite contrary to the reality, of proclaiming his accuracy and love of order on all occasions with Ciceronian eloquence. Only when it became necessary to spend days, hours, sometimes weeks, in finding something necessary and all efforts remained fruitless, did he adopt a different tone, and the innocent were made to bear the blame. "Yes, yes," was the complaint, "that's a misfortune! Nothing is permitted to remain where I put it; everything is moved about; everything is done to vex me; O men, men!" But his servants knew the good-natured grumbler; let him growl to his heart's content, and—in a few minutes all would be forgotten, until another occasion brought with it a renewal of the scene.

He often made merry over his illegible handwriting and excused him-

6. *Ibid.*

self by saying: "Life is too short to paint letters or notes; and prettier notes would scarcely help me out of needs."

The whole forenoon, from the first ray of light till the meal hour, was devoted to mechanical labor, i.e., to transcribing; the rest of the day was given to thought and the ordering of ideas. Hardly had he put the last bit in his mouth before he began his customary promenade, unless he had some other excursion *in petto*; that is to say, he hurried in double-quick time several times around the city, as if urged on by a goad; and this, let the weather be what it might.

At the beginning of the year 1804 Beethoven was completing the final copy of the Third Symphony. On January 4 he wrote to Johann Friedrich Rochlitz, the founder and editor of the Leipzig *Allgemeine musikalische Zeitung*, that he was starting to work on the adaption of a French libretto; this was Joseph Sonnleithner's translation into German of Bouilly's *Léonore, ou L'Amour conjugal*. During the first half of this year work was completed on the Piano Sonata, Op. 53, dedicated to Count Waldstein, and the Concerto for Violin, Cello, and Piano, Op. 56.[7] That summer he was occupied with work on the Piano Sonatas, Opp. 54 and 57, the "Appassionata."

Meanwhile Beethoven's orchestra music was beginning at last to receive repeated performances. Thayer writes:[8]

> It was to the discredit of Vienna, where instrumental performers of rare ability so abounded, that for several years regular public orchestral concerts, save those at the Augarten in the summer, had been abandoned. Sensible of this, the bankers Würth and Fellner during the winter of 1803-04 "had gathered together on all Sunday mornings a select company [nearly all dilettanti] for concerts restricted for the greater part to pieces for full orchestra such as symphonies [among them Beethoven's First and Second], overtures, concertos, which they played in really admirable style ...." Thus the correspondent of the Allgemeine musikalische Zeitung. In these concerts Clement of the Theater-an-der-Wien was director.

These concerts were renewed in 1805, and on February 13 the Third Symphony received its first semi-public performance. This was followed by a full, public performance on April 7th, which Beethoven conducted.

Now Beethoven's compositional labors had turned full force to the completion of his opera *Leonore*—or *Fidelio*, as it was billed for its first performance.[9] Sketches were completed by June, 1805, and the writing-

---

7. According to Schindler, the piano part was written for Beethoven's pupil, Archduke Rudolph, half-brother of Emperor Francis I.

8. Thayer, *op. cit.*, pp. 374-75.

9. At the insistence of the theatre directors, against Beethoven's wishes.

out was the work of his summer sojourn in outlying Hetzendorf. In September he returned to the city to prepare the music for rehearsals; the performance was set for November 20. It was a time of severe strain, due to rushing through parts for copyists, as well as endless casting and rehearsal details. At the same time, the city was in a state of tension due to the advance of Napoleon's army. The aristocracy, who could normally be counted on to appreciate each of the composer's new creations, were fleeing the city. The vanguard of the French army entered Vienna on November 13, a week before the performance. The result was that the opera played for three consecutive nights to scanty audiences, the majority of whom were the occupying French, and then closed down.

The first overture that Beethoven wrote for Leonore (*Leonore* No. 1, Op. 138) had already been performed privately and judged too light, whereupon he wrote a second, more dynamic one (*Leonore* No. 2), which was used at these performances. Besides the *Leonore* music, Beethoven had sketched and started work on his Piano Concerto in G, Op. 58, before the end of the year.

Now we can consider the early sketches for the Fifth Symphony, which, because of their proximity to sketches for some of the works mentioned above, may be safely dated 1804–05. In the first set[10] there are ideas for the first and third movements alongside some early drafts for the first five numbers of *Leonore*. There is an isolated sketch for the opening bars of the Fourth Piano Concerto. Finally there are sketches for the revision of the first two pieces in the oratorio *Christus am Ölberg*, a revision Beethoven undertook in 1804, as we know from a letter to the publishers, Breitkopf & Härtel.[11]

A second set of sketches[12] contains ideas for the first and second movements and an unused idea for the finale. There are also extended sketches for the concerto and a fragment for the terzett "Gut, Söhnchen, gut," which concludes the original first act of *Leonore*.

A later set of sheets has more developed ideas for the second and third movements, alongside sketches for *Leonore* Overture No. 1.[13] Thus, as we will examine more in detail in a separate section, Beethoven had projected clear ideas for at least three of the four symphony movements by the fall of 1805.

10. Gustav Nottebohm, *Ein Skizzenbuch von Beethoven aus dem Jahre 1803*, Leipzig, 1880, pp. 70–71.

11. See Emily Anderson, *Letters of Beethoven*, London, 1961, p. 116.

12. Gustav Nottebohm, *Beethoveniana*, Leipzig, 1872, pp. 10–16. In all subsequent references, this will be abbreviated as *NBv*.

13. *NBv.*, pp. 62–65.

The year 1806, however, was to bring new interruptions in the creation of the Fifth Symphony. First, Beethoven was advised by his friends to remodel his opera. This he had probably started to do (with the help of Stephan von Breuning, who revised the libretto) before the end of 1805, for the second version of *Leonore-Fidelio* was performed on March 29, 1806, with a new overture, *Leonore* No. 3.

Since 1804 Beethoven had been contemplating a return to quartet writing. Now with striking speed he wrote the three "Razumovsky" Quartets, Op. 59, one right after another. No. 1, according to the autograph, was "begun" on May 26, a date that probably refers to the final working-out, since all three were completed by the late fall.

The work of the second half-year centered around the Fourth Symphony and the Violin Concerto. On the autograph of the symphony Beethoven wrote "Sinfonia 4ta, 1806. L. v. Bthvn." No sketches have survived, but it is clear that Beethoven composed rapidly, for on September 3 he wrote from Silesia to the publishers, Breitkopf & Härtel, offering them a number of works, including a new symphony, which he said he could send immediately. Back in Vienna, he wrote again to the publishers on November 18 and made another offer of works but added, "I cannot give you the promised symphony yet—because a gentleman of quality has taken it from me, but I have the privilege of publishing it in half a year." The gentleman was doubtless Count Oppersdorff, to whom the symphony was eventually dedicated. This nobleman also figures in the later history of the Fifth Symphony, as we shall see.

In the fall Beethoven was rushing to completion his Violin Concerto, which was performed on December 23. Sketches for the work appear alongside those for the Cello Sonata in A major and the Fifth Symphony.[14] These last are in an advanced state and include studies for the bridge between the third movement and the finale. They may be dated late 1806 or, more likely, 1807, the year in which the main work on the symphony was done.

A new rush job interfered in the first part of this year. The Overture to *Coriolan* was included in a pair of concerts given at the house of Prince Lobkowitz in early March for the composer's benefit. Also played were his first four symphonies, a piano concerto[15] and some airs from the opera *Fidelio*, according to a report in the *Journal des Luxus und der Moden*. We know that the overture was also played in the same period at

14. Nottebohm, *Zweite Beethoveniana*, Leipzig, 1887, pp. 528–34. In all subsequent references, this will be abbreviated as *NzBv*.

15. A first semi-public performance of No. 4.

the house of Prince Lichnowsky.

The next interruption was an invitation from Prince Nikolaus Esterhazy to write a mass in honor of his wife, for performance in September on her name-day. Work on the symphony proceeded simultaneously with the completion of this commission during the early summer, first in Baden, then in Heiligenstadt. Also in the second half of the year, Beethoven had begun to compose his Sixth Symphony in earnest, sketches for which exist as early as 1804.

A new concert series was inaugurated during the year, which made it possible for Beethoven's music to be heard again in concerts other than the summer offerings led by the violinist Schuppanzigh or the hastily put together benefit and charity concerts in the winter. It was called *Liebhaber-Concert*, concert of music-lovers. Most of the orchestra members were dilettanti and the audience of the nobility. Reports of these concerts indicate that during a series of twenty concerts in 1807–08 the Second Symphony, *Prometheus* Overture, Third Symphony, *Coriolan* Overture, and Fourth Symphony were heard, with the composer presumably directing all his own works. Beethoven also contributed his services to three concerts for public charities: on November 15, 1807, April 13 and November 15, 1808, during which the Fourth Symphony, *Coriolan* Overture, and one of his piano concertos were played. As a result of these last services Court Councillor Joseph Hartl, who was both theatre director and supervisor of public charities, gave Beethoven what he had been wanting for more than a year, the use of the Theater-an-der-Wien for a benefit concert for himself. The date was set for December 22, and the history of compositions in 1808 centers around the preparation of new works for this important event.

We return now to Count Oppersdorff. In the summer of 1806 Beethoven apparently took no summer lodgings, but by September he had made a trip to Silesia to visit Prince Lichnowsky. Count Oppersdorff was himself a music-lover and cared enough about the art to have an orchestra at his castle in Upper Silesia, about a day's ride from Lichnowsky's. Beethoven and the Prince were invited to visit the Count, on which occasion there was a performance of the Second Symphony. As we know from the correspondence with his publishers, Beethoven gave the Count the manuscript of the Fourth Symphony before his return to Vienna; consequently he was unable to send it to them.[16] A receipt in Beethoven's hand, dated February 13, 1807, shows that the Symphony was com-

16. In the end, it was not published by this concern but by the Bureau des Arts et d'Industrie, Vienna, in 1808.

missioned by the Count, who paid him 500 florins, kept the score for the conventional six-month period, and received the dedication. We trace these negotiations in such detail because the sequel is not altogether clear.

Stimulated by this commission, the Count requested sponsorship of the next symphony. By March, 1808 he was evidently impatient, for Beethoven wrote to him:

> * * * I only want to inform you that *your symphony* has long been ready, and I will now send it to you by the next post—You may retain 50 florins, for the copying, which I will have done for you, will cost that sum at least—In case you do not want the symphony, however, let me know it before the next post—In case you accept it, rejoice me as soon as possible with the 300 fl. still due me. *The last movement in the symphony i*s with 3 trombones and flautini [piccolo]—though not with 3 kettledrums, but will make more noise than 6 kettledrums and better noise at that.

This letter shows that Beethoven and the Count had discussed instrumentation and also that Beethoven was in real need of money. It appears that the price of the symphony was again 500 florins; a second receipt shows that Beethoven received 200 florins in June, 1807 and a further 150 florins on March 29, 1808. But the Count was destined to wait for the score in vain; Beethoven wrote him on November 1st:[17]

> Best Count!
> You will look at me in a false light, but necessity compelled me to sell to someone else the symphony which was written for you and another as well * * *

This "someone else" was Breitkopf & Härtel, with whom he had resumed negotiations. On September 14 he received 100 ducats in gold from the firm for five new works: the Fifth Symphony, Sixth Symphony, two Trios, Op. 70, and the Cello Sonata, Op. 69.

These were the important works that were completed in 1808. But another larger work was written before the end of the year, specifically for Beethoven's benefit concert of December 22. Already projected for the program were the Fifth and Sixth Symphonies, the Fourth Piano Concerto, with Beethoven as soloist, a piano improvisation by the composer, an aria and two excerpts from the Mass in C! Yet Beethoven, in consultation with his friends, was concerned that the fourth movement of the Fifth Symphony would not be suitable as a finale to the program because by then the audience would be too tired to appreciate it. Therefore in

17. For both letters to Oppersdorff in full, see Thayer, *op. cit.*, pp. 432–34.

great haste he wrote a piece to make a flashy and brilliant finish: the Fantasia for Pianoforte, Orchestra and Chorus, Op. 80.

The concert was announced on December 17 in the *Wiener Zeitung,* with the numbering of the two symphonies inexplicably reversed, as follows:

MUSICAL AKADEMIE

On Thursday, December 22, Ludwig van Beethoven will have the honor to give a musical *Akademie* in the R.I. Priv. Theater-an-der-Wien. All the pieces are of his composition, entirely new, and not yet heard in public ... First Part: 1, A Symphony, entitled: "A Recollection of Country Life," in F major (No. 5). 2, Aria. 3, Hymn with Latin text, composed in the church style with chorus and solos. 4, Pianoforte Concerto played by himself.

Second Part. 1, Grand Symphony in C minor (No. 6). 2, Sanctus, with Latin text composed in the church style with chorus and solos. 3, Fantasia for Pianoforte alone. 4, Fantasia for the Pianoforte which ends with the gradual entrance of the entire orchestra and the introduction of choruses as a finale.

Boxes and reserved seats are to be had in the Krugerstrasse No. 1074, first story. Beginning at half past six o'clock.

With such a gargantuan program of entirely new music it is not surprising that there were performance difficulties, particularly in the Choral Fantasia, which had been completed so late that it had received hardly any rehearsal. Relations between composer and orchestra were already strained because of a misunderstanding that had occurred in the preparation of the recent concert of November 15. The aria chosen was *Ah, perfido! spergiuro,* Op. 65; a quarrel in rehearsal forced a last minute change of soprano soloist.[18] The accounts of the concert reflect these difficulties. Reichardt describes the scene:[19]

I accepted the kind offer of Prince Lobkowitz to let me sit in his box with hearty thanks. There we continued, in the bitterest cold, too, from half past six to half past ten, and experienced the truth that one can easily have too much of a good thing—and still more of a loud. Nevertheless, I could no more leave the box before the end than could the exceedingly good-natured and delicate Prince, for the box was in the first balcony near the stage, so that the orchestra with Beethoven in the middle conducting it was below us and near at hand; thus many a failure in the performance

18. The veteran Anna Pauline Milder was replaced by a young, inexperienced singer, Josephine Killitschgy.

19. Johann Friedrich Reichardt (1752-1814) was a German composer and writer. His *Vertraute Briefe* describe musical life in Vienna in 1808-09. See Thayer, *op. cit.,* p. 448.

vexed our patience in the highest degree. Poor Beethoven, who from this, his own concert, was having the first and only scant profit that he could find in a whole year, had found in the rehearsals and performance a lot of opposition and almost no support. Singers and orchestra were composed of heterogeneous elements, and it had been found impossible to get a single full rehearsal for all the pieces to be performed, all filled with the greatest difficulties.

In a letter to Breitkopf & Härtel dated January 7, 1809, Beethoven complained of the bad conditions at the theatre and the musical elements with which he had had to struggle. He writes:[20]

> Notwithstanding the fact that several mistakes were made, which I could not help, the public accepted everything enthusiastically—Nevertheless, scribblers from here will certainly not fail again to send miserable stuff against me in the Musikalische Zeitung—The musicians were particularly angry because when a blunder was made through carelessness in the simplest, plainest place in the world, I stopped them suddenly and loudly called out "Once again"—Such a thing had never happened to them before. The public showed its enjoyment of this—

The Leipzig *Allgemeine musikalische Zeitung*[21] wisely suspended judgment of this music after a single hearing and thereby showed simultaneously its respect for Beethoven and its editorial honesty.

On January 23, 1809, the symphony received its second performance at a Gewandhaus concert in Leipzig; this time there was a review, the first serious one that the work had received, by Rochlitz, the AmZ editor.[22] We quote in part:

> It was first performed at an extraordinary concert by Mr. Tietz of Dresden at which the execution was not good due to the great difficulties involved. The next performance at a weekly concert went very well (with the exception of a few details) and was received enthusiastically. The first movement is a very serious, somewhat gloomy yet fiery allegro, noble both in feeling and in the working-out of idea, which is handled firmly and evenly, simply with a lot of originality, strength and consistency—a worthy movement which offers rich pleasure even to those who cling to the old way of composing a big symphony.

The second movement was admired for its originality "composed of the most heterogeneous ideas—from the gently fanciful to the rough march-like"; the scherzando despite its wonderful whims was found less

20. Thayer, *op. cit.*, p. 454. This was undoubtedly the mishap in the Choral Fantasia; for other accounts of this incident, see Thayer, pp. 448–49.

21. XI (January, 1809), 267–68.

22. XI (April, 1809), 433–35. See p. 150.

pleasing and judged almost impossible for a large orchestra to perform; and the finale was likened to a tempestuous explosion of powerful fantasy, unprecedented in symphonic writing.

The autograph of the Fifth Symphony is in the Berlin State Library. A limited-edition facsimile was made by G. Schünemann and published by Staercke in Berlin in 1942. That editor has written the following note concerning the autograph:[23]

> On the first page of the "5th" Beethoven has written "Sinfonie di L. v. Beethoven." with a red chalk pencil. He was inclined to use red chalk for his last notations. By the same token this represented the final stage of his creative work. He had held on to this habit since his youth * * * Unfortunately the thick pencil blurred easily. Beethoven mentioned this to Sebastian Mayer:[24] "Anything that is written with red pencil must be touched up by the copyist with ink, otherwise it fades!" The inscription of the "Fifth" is indeed "faded," but otherwise the big, broad marks in red pencil are for the most part preserved.
>
> On the first page of the autograph there is another indication for the copyist: "Flauti, Oboe, Clarinetti, Fagotti, Corni tutti obligati." The copyist is thus informed that all winds are handled independently and not bound to the strings as in many of the works of contemporaries. On the last page Beethoven gives the copyist the following instruction: "Copy in the piccolo and trombone parts at the end after all the other parts have been copied. The sign ₵ in the first section leads to ₵ in the second section when it occurs." Despite ample sketchwork Beethoven himself made corrections on and on into the final copy. He had to cross out so much that he had to lay out a system of his own to use. He writes "aus," which means "omit," and then crosses it out. Occasionally the word "aus" gets written over repeatedly first with ink, then red pencil, then lead pencil. One also finds "gut" and "meilleur" and "bleibt" ("good," "better," "remains"). These indications can also be found crossed out or restored. Specifically in the "Fifth" there are many passages which Beethoven was constantly improving and polishing. Especially difficult was the problem that he had set for himself of the transition to the last movement. After many attempts, which can be seen in his sketchbooks,[25] he was still reworking it in his final copy. The original instrumentation which included winds was crossed out. Only the violins retained the passage expressing motion gradually and steadily increasing and intensifying, always gaining in power, which had been planned from the first sketches.
>
> It cannot have been easy to read and copy those pages under Beethoven's supervision. And Beethoven also had much difficulty with his copyists, who were not exactly competing eagerly for this work. His favorite was

23. *Musiker-Handschriften von Bach bis Schumann*, Berlin, 1936, pp. 68–69.
24. Friedrich Sebastian Mayer, who married Mozart's sister-in-law, Josepha Weber, was an actor and singer, the original Pizarro in *Leonore*.
25. Most of these sheets are in the Berlin State Library.

and remained the copyist Schlemmer,[26] who was very familiar with his corrections and abbreviations.

The Symphony was published in April, 1809[27] and dedicated

à son Altesse Sérénissime
Monseigneur le Prince régnant de Lobkowitz
Duc de Raudnitz
et
A son Excellence Monsieur le Comte de Rasumoffsky
par
Louis van Beethoven[28]

Not Count Oppersdorff, about whom we know nothing more, but rather an unusual double dedication. Prince Franz Joseph Lobkowitz (1772–1816) had maintained an orchestra in his splendid Vienna palace since 1796 and played the violin himself. He was one of Beethoven's most generous patrons and in 1809 joined with Archduke Rudolph and Prince Kinsky to guarantee the composer a yearly income to prevent his leaving Vienna. Lobkowitz received the dedications also to Opp. 18, 55, 56, 74 and 98. Count Andreas Kyrillovitsch Razumovsky (1752–1836) had been since 1792 the Russian Ambassador to Vienna. Also a violinist, he established a resident quartet in 1808 which played for six years. To him were dedicated also the Quartets, Op. 59.

In a letter dated March 4, 1809 Beethoven indicated this joint dedication to his publishers with instructions that it was to apply to both the Fifth and Sixth Symphonies. He added:

> Tomorrow you will receive particulars of some minor corrections I made during the performances of the symphonies—for when I gave them to you, I had not yet heard either of them—and one should not pretend to be so divine as not to correct things here and there in one's works.

Unfortunately the list of corrections was not sent until March 28, too late for the first issue, but in time for the second issue later in the year. The most important of these changes was the sustaining of the D at m. 4 (first movement) for an extra measure (and in similar statements at mm. 23, 127, 251, and 481).

Beethoven's problems with those entrusted to bring his works to print is well illustrated by his letter to Leipzig of November 2nd:[29]

26. Alan Tyson doubts that Schlemmer was the copyist here. See *The Beethoven Companion*, London, 1971, p. 471, fn. 1.

27. Instrumental parts only. The full score was published in 1826.

28. See Kinsky, *op. cit.*, p. 159.

29. Thayer, *op. cit.*, p. 460.

* * * why is this very fine edition not without inaccuracies???? Why did you not send me first a copy to check, as I have so often asked you to do? Errors creep into every copy, but they are errors which any competent proof-reader can correct, although indeed I am almost certain that there are few, if any, mistakes in the copy I sent you. It is impossible always to send copies in my own handwriting. But I checked the trios and symphonies so carefully that with more accurate proofreading there should have been very few mistakes and, if any, only unimportant ones—I am rather annoyed about this—Here is the list. As poets and writers, when they can't be on the spot where their works are being produced, have a list of errata printed, you must do the same thing—and I will make out the list here—[30]

Unfortunately this list has not survived. But in a following section we give a revealing list of discrepancies compiled by Heinrich Schenker between the autograph and later editions.

One error was not corrected until many years later. In a postscript to a long letter to his publishers dated August 21, 1810, Beethoven writes:[31]

... I have found another error in the Symphony in C minor, namely, in the third movement in ¾ time where, after the ♮ ♮ ♮ the minor returns again, it reads (I just take the bass part) thus:

The two measures marked by a ✕ are redundant and must be stricken out, of course also in all the parts that are pausing.

The history of this error is well summarized in Donald Francis Tovey's essay on the Symphony.[32]

30. Anderson, *op. cit.*, p. 246.
31. Thayer, *op. cit.*, p. 500.
32. See p. 148.

THE SCORE
OF THE SYMPHONY

INSTRUMENTATION

Piccolo

2 Flutes

2 Oboes

2 Clarinets, in B♭ and C

2 Bassoons

Contrabassoon

2 Horns, in E♭ and C

2 Trumpets in C

3 Trombones

Timpani

Violin I

Violin II

Viola

Cello

Double Bass

SYMPHONY NO. 5 IN C MINOR

I: Allegro con brio

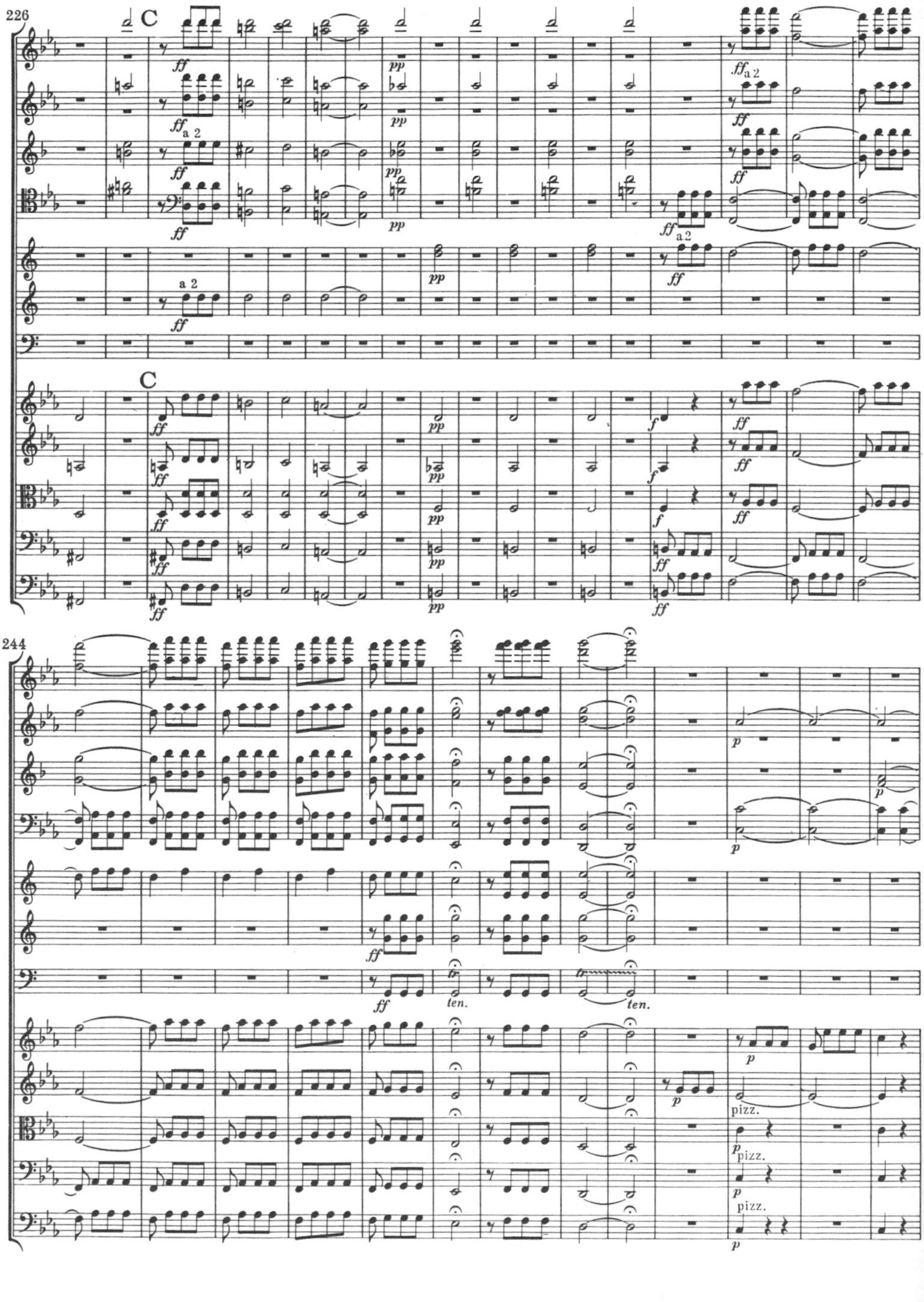
226
C
ff
a 2
pp
C
f
244
p
ten.
tr
pizz.

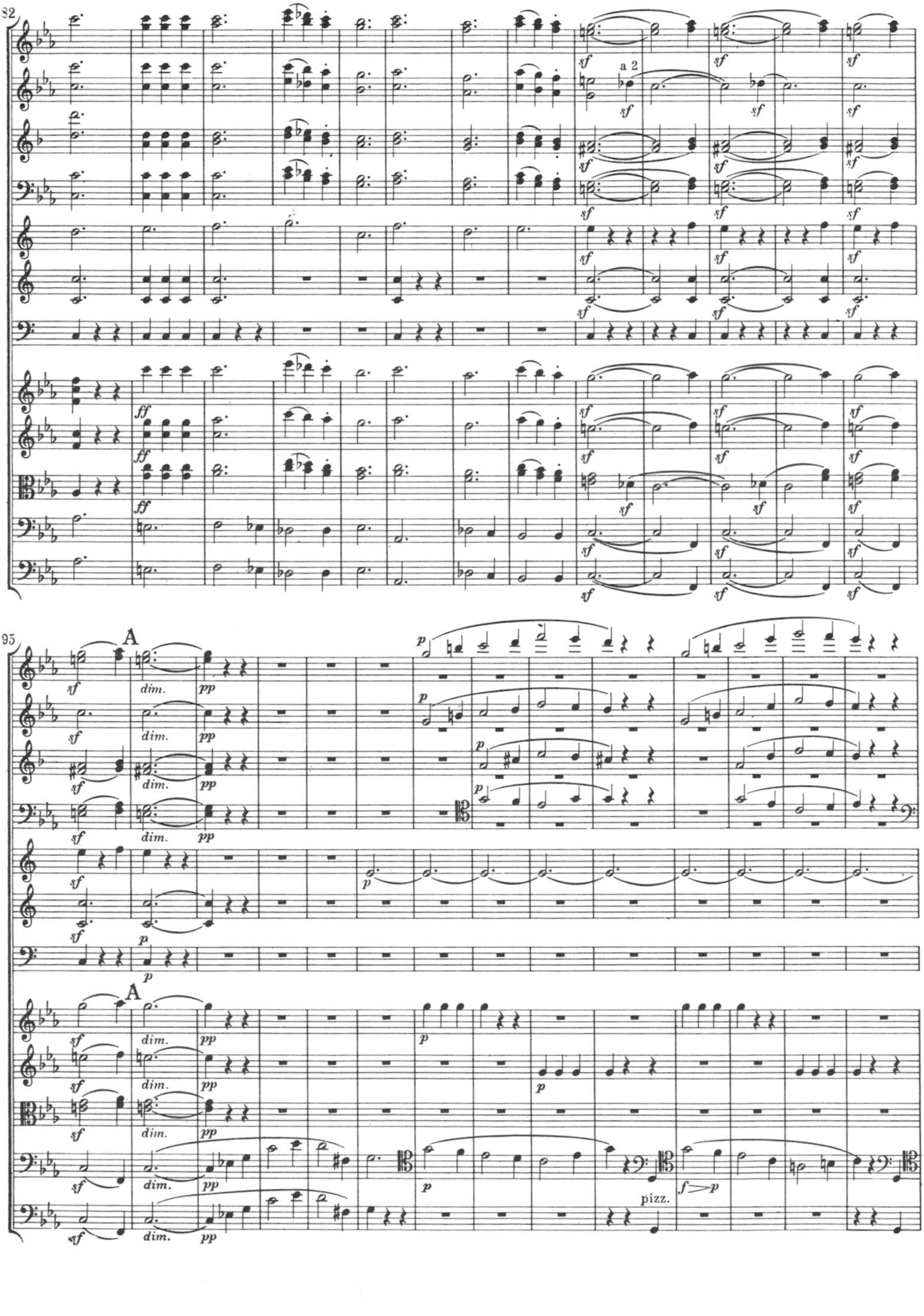
82
a 2
95
A
A
dim.
pp
pizz.

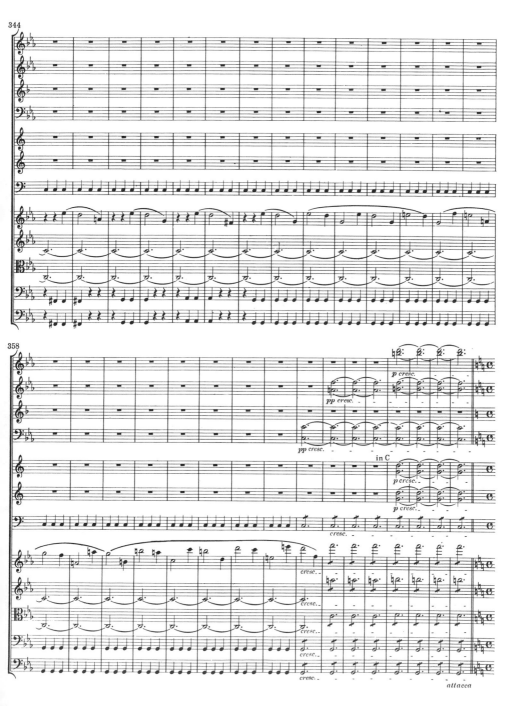

IV: Allegro

98

160

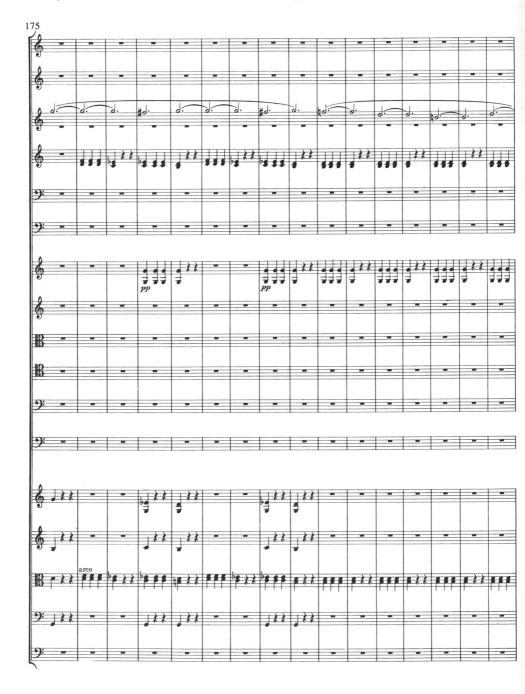

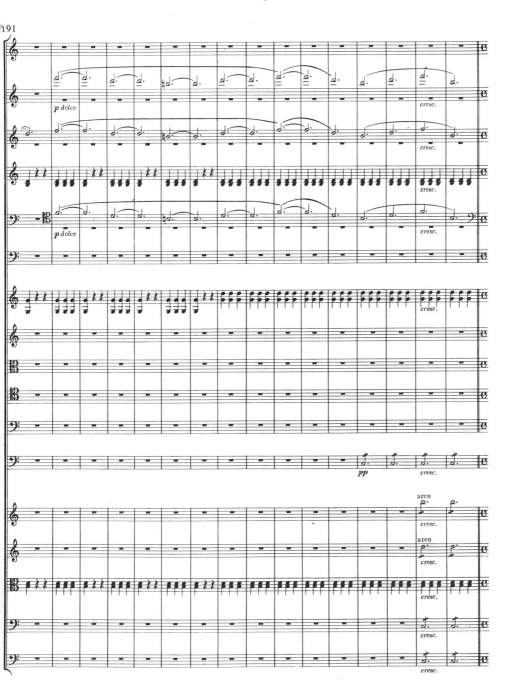

223

229

283

309

330

347

sempre più Allegro

sempre più Allegro

367

415

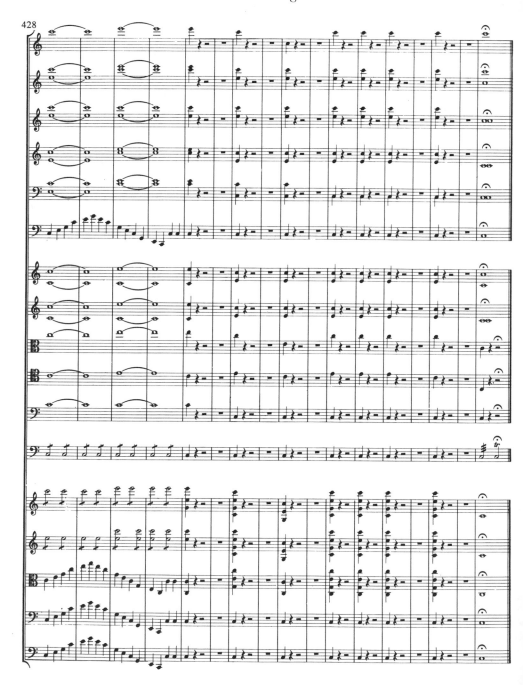

The Sketches

The sketches for the Fifth Symphony that have survived were almost all brought to light by Gustav Nottebohm. Most of them are to be found on loose sheets, but a few appear in the latter part of the so-called *Eroica Sketchbook*. We will take them up movement by movement. Three observations should be made: first, Nottebohm published only selected extracts from the sketches, as shown by his indication "etc."; second, Beethoven's habit in sketching was not only to fill up page after page but often to go back and fill in blank areas of earlier pages, so that the order of sketches is not certain; and third, key signatures and clefs have to be assumed in the subsequent staves of a given sketch.

FIRST MOVEMENT

Ex. 1

In this sketch[1] the first twenty measures outline the basic course of the melody; see m. 21 in the score. The addition of a measure in the score is made by the held D from m. 4 to 5, a correction that Beethoven did not make until after he had heard the first performance.[2]

The sketch shows the origin of that important stepwise descending figure which, alternating with its inversion, is first used in m. 14ff., to lead to the half-cadence in m. 21. However, in m. 7 of the sketch we find it already leading from the third to the tonic, Eb–D–C. The softness of this is in sharp contrast to the final version where the drop of the third is in direct relation to the opening motive:

Ex. 2

After m. 20, the difference between the sketch and the final version is striking. In the former the key of Eb is introduced immediately with the second subject. Its derivation, rhythmic and melodic, from the first subject is thus more emphasized; on the other hand, the degree of contrast provided by the second subject—tonally, texturally, and melodically—is nowhere near as strong as in the final version, when its appearance has been preceded by over 50 measures of solid C-minor expression (see mm. 1-58 in the score). Furthermore, in the sketch the second key is only suggested, rather than established, since the melody of the second subject is immediately restated in C minor. The sketch then suggests not only a longer transition section but also a longer exposition section, rather than the concise 124 measures of the final version.

Another sketch shows an early working-out of the rhythmic germ in G minor[3]:

Ex. 3

Then comes an ascending use of the rhythmic figure in C minor over a

1. *Ein Skizzenbuch, op. cit.*, p. 71.
2. Similarly mm. 24, 128, 252, and 482 are not to be found in the autograph.
3. *NBv.*, p. 10.

dominant pedal,[4] similar to the rise over the tonic pedal to be found in mm. 33 ff. of the score:

Ex. 4

The next sketch works the motive again imitatively and sequentially and again shows the inclination to dip from the tonic into the relative major and back again. Note the indication "presto" under "Sinfonia. Allegro primo."[5]

Ex. 5

The alternating drop of a third and rise of a second in the last four

4. *NBv.*, p. 11.
5. *NBv.*

measures anticipate the long sequence in the coda, which is prepared in
m. 406 and starts in m. 407 of the score.

   After the double bar comes another rising line, based on the central
rhythmic germ, this time under a tonic pedal. One is reminded of the
upper tonic pedal in the coda, mm. 374 ff. In the latter the C pushes first
to the lowered second, Db (m. 382). This instinct to push from C up a
half-step is demonstrated in both pedal-point passages from the sketches.

SECOND MOVEMENT

Ex. 6

This sketch[6] shows four measures of the first melody in a crude state,
with an almost literal repetition of the opening figure a step higher. This
is followed by the second melody, which in eight measures evidently
modulates to C minor, rather than to C major as in the final version.
Nine measures follow in which the melody, now clearly in C major,
modulates back immediately to the tonic, Ab major. Beethoven labels
the opening melody "Andante quasi Menuetto" and the second melody
"quasi Trio"; the latter's answer is to be stated by the brass. (See the

   6. *NBv.*, p. 14.

orchestration of mm. 32 ff.) In the final version the tutti scoring was already applied in the preceding cadence, mm. 29–31. Thus a minuet section is implied in A♭ major to be followed by a trio section with the form, in keys: |: A♭ – C :|: C – A♭ :| No hint as yet of the idea of theme and variations.

Ex. 7

Ex. 8

The second set of sketches[7] show a more advanced treatment of the main melody. The first three staves represent a transition to a return statement of the subject. Beethoven was to use these triplet figures in the digression of his second variation (mm. 160 ff. in the score). The snatch of reprise (last measure of the sheet labelled "No. 2" by Nottebohm) is developed as a motive in sheet "No. 3" in a culminating kind of statement which found realisation in the coda, mm. 229 ff. in the score. This rhythmic variation, 𝄽 𝅘𝅥 𝅘𝅥𝅮𝅘𝅥𝅮𝅘𝅥𝅮𝅘𝅥𝅮 , is first introduced in the final version starting at m. 127, and sparks a development through to m. 147. It is the opening idea of the "Più mosso" section of the coda (mm. 205 ff.) before its culmination, which starts at m. 229, as mentioned above. Finally, the sketch shows that the emphasis on the falling third of the theme— E♭–C—was already in the composer's mind (mm. 5–10 in "No. 3"); it is this interval which was to find such extensive elaboration within each version of the melody in its final form.

Ex. 9

7. *NBv.*, p. 63.

Ex. 10

This last fragment[8] shows the main theme well advanced, with the dotted rhythm already applied to mm. 4 and 5 and the rhythm ♫|♩♬ now used to initiate the theme.

THIRD AND FOURTH MOVEMENTS

The sketches for the third movement are the most extensive of the four. They show that Beethoven originally had in mind a closed movement rather than one connected to and acting as a bridge to the finale.[9]

The first subject, without upbeat, is shown in an early version, with its eight measures repeated literally. The second subject follows (m. 17) *forte*, modulates to E♭ minor and then to D♭ major. Starting at m. 44 the first subject takes over and modulates back to C minor, cadencing on the dominant (m. 58). The first section of the trio follows, again without upbeat, and cadences on C.

A later set of sketches shows transformed versions of the opening themes of the C minor and C major sections and an early suggestion of the bridge from the third to fourth movement.[10]

Ex. 11

(No. 1)

"No. 1" gives the latter part of the trio melody, followed directly without transition by the C minor melody. Compare the cadence at m. 196 and what follows: the repeat of the trio answer, which acts as a transition to the C-minor section, mm. 197–235.

"No. 4" and "No. 5" form a sketch for a transition from the section in C minor to that in C major. Here Beethoven is experimenting with the first subject over an A♭ pedal, but not yet in connection with the bridge between movements.

8. *NzBv.*, p. 534.
9. *Skizzenbuch, op. cit.*, p. 70.
10. *NBv.*, pp. 62–64.

    "No. 6" shows a cadence to the trio section in which the falling motive has been polished from the form in "No. 1" to and put in a counterpoint against the beginning of the subject.

    On the reverse side of the last page is the first indication of a bridge between the triple rhythm of the third movement and the duple of the finale.[11] The repeated-note theme cadences in C *pianissimo*, and its rhythm is taken over by a tonic pedal, which for nine measures remains in triple time before shifting to the duple time of the finale.

Ex. 15

Our last set of sketches (which includes the final fragment for the second movement, already given) belong to a later period. While the sketches discussed so far may be dated probably 1804–05, the following belong to the year 1806–07.

The first shows a four-measure introduction to the opening theme which, if used, would have robbed the rising figure of its light, upbeat characteristic.[12]

Ex. 16

Notice that the theme now has a fermata after the first statement and that the variation in its repetition is already implied (mm. 1–8 versus 9–18 in the score).

Nottebohm shows one short sketch and one long one for the bridge between the third and last movement:

11. *NBv.*, p. 64.
12. *NzBv.*, p. 528.

Ex. 17

Ex. 18

The second one, for the first eighteen measures, corresponds rhythmically to the printed score (see mm. 322–39). From here on the sketched version is longer (by nine measures) and implies a harmonic sequence downward until the final dominant expression, in contrast to the concentrated use of the initial rhythmic motive in rising sequence, which occurs in the final version.

Ex. 19

Then follows this sketch for the bridge in the middle of the finale, from the third movement reprise to the recapitulation.[13] These thirteen measures on the dominant differ from the equivalent twenty-two measures in the score (mm. 184–206) first and foremost in the way they break, half way through, into the duple rhythm to come, with downward rushes reminiscent of the *Leonore* Overtures, which Beethoven had just composed.

One last point should be made concerning sketches for the finale. A sketch from the earlier years shows that Beethoven did not originally have in mind a triumphant C-major allegro idea. Along with first attempts for the first two movements there is a beginning marked "l'ultimo pezzo" (the last piece), in C minor and six-eight time.[14]

Ex. 20

13. *NzBv.*, p. 530.
14. *NBv.*, p. 15.

Walter Riezler has made an interesting summary of the implications in tonal terms for the symphony as a whole of these two contrasting ways of handling the finale:[15]

> The tremendous energy of the last movement ensures the unity of the work. Needless to say, it had to be different from the first movement; not only is its brilliant major opposed to its more sombre minor, but its close-packed breadth contrasts with the almost excessive tension and compactness of the other movement. It was just this compactness that called for a *dénouement* of this kind after the two middle movements, which themselves had to be different—and different in this very way—from the first and the last.
>
> The Andante, with its sense of relaxation, is the only slow movement that would be tolerable after the opening movement. The third, with its almost spectral groping, points to a *dénouement* that could not well be other than it is. The fact that it runs into the last movement without a break shows quite clearly the close inward relationship of the two; and this relationship is reaffirmed by the much discussed re-introduction of the theme in the finale. The resulting contrast certainly has a striking effect, and it enabled the composer to avoid the risk of the jubilant tone of the finale becoming monotonous. But if there were no other relationship, the exciting effect of this re-introduction would be incomprehensible. Actually it has an effect of inevitability: the gloom and the ghostly visitants have not been finally exorcized by the radiance of the finale. When the strains of the third movement are heard again, the full depth of the abyss from which triumph has emerged is brought clearly home to us. The similarity of the motives in different movements, which is so often referred to, is not in itself proof of the unity of the work as a whole. That the three throbbing beats of the first motive reappear in the third movement is obvious, and they may be heard here and there even in the finale. And in the C-major passage of the Andante, which has no formal close, we can hear in anticipation the triumphant strains of the finale. Beethoven would perhaps not have permitted himself this musical anacoluthon had he not intended its logical fulfillment in the last movement. The latter was originally planned on entirely different lines, i.e., as a passionate minor movement; this passage in the Andante was then intended to have a definite close.

15. *Beethoven.*, transl. G. D. H. Pidcock, London, 1938, pp. 148–49.

Textual Note

[The score reprinted here is based on that published by Breitkopf & Härtel in the Complete Edition of Beethoven's works (1864–67). It has been modified in the light of the discrepancies found by Heinrich Schenker between the printed scores and Beethoven's autograph. Schenker's list of these discrepancies[1] follows, along with his comments on the autograph and the sketches that have not already been discussed in his preceding section. See pp. 164–82.]

See pp. 164–82.

FIRST MOVEMENT

The metronome marking $\mathbf{\mathit{d}}$ = 108 is not present in the autograph: it was added subsequently to the parts and the score.[2] In this connection Nottebohm writes in his *Beethoveniana*, p. 135: "Some of Beethoven's tempo indications will be found not completely appropriate to the character of a given piece. Thus some symphonic movements seem to us marked too fast. This phenomenon may perhaps be explained by the supposition that Beethoven established the metronome marks at the piano and arrived at conclusions that would have been difficult for him to carry out in the concert hall. Nevertheless the existing markings can prevent many misconceptions and serve as a basis for discussion in doubtful or controversial cases. . . . Beethoven's indication for the first movement of the C-minor Symphony (Allegro con brio, $\mathbf{\mathit{d}}$ = 108) refutes Schindler's testimony[3] that for the first five measures Beethoven established a slower tempo, namely $\mathbf{\mathit{d}}$ = 126, almost an Andante con moto. If Beethoven had intended the tempo change, he would certainly have indicated it with a metronome mark."

The autograph shows that a great deal of work was done on many passages, often more than would ordinarily be described as "finishing

---

1. From *Der Tonwille*, V (1923), 10–13, 39–41; VI (1923), 18–20, 29–31. Reprinted with permission of Universal Edition A. G., Vienna. Translation by the editor and F. John Adams, Jr.

2. The metronome marks for the first eight symphonies originally appeared in a supplement to the Leipzig *Allgemeine musikalische Zeitung*, December 17, 1817. [*Editor*]

3. Nottebohm gives the reference: Biography, 1st ed., p. 241. [*Editor*]

touches." That the score lacked mm. 5, 24, 127, 252, and 482 has been mentioned in connection with Example 3[4]. Many other measures in the score can be clearly seen to have been inserted. This is the case with mm. 22-23 (the introductory motto of the consequent: Example 3, Id); originally the contents of the fermata continued in m. 25 (as the fourth measure of a group) without that loud exclamation. Further insertions will best be mentioned as we come to them.

At mm. 34 ff. (and correspondingly at mm. 277 ff.) basic corrections were made for Vn. II and Va. There was much concern at mm. 48 ff. and 292 ff. over the arpeggiation of the four-note chord; here are some of the attempts:

The notational form that the composer used consistently for this figure:  is a better reflection of the motive than the version in more recent editions: [music notation] .

In the first three repetitions, starting at m. 63, there was originally a different order of instruments: Cl.-Fl., Vn.I -Ob., Vn.I -Fl.

The bowing marks in the autograph from m. 83 on are especially significant; the lower marks in the following example show the original bowing:

Afterwards, a measure was inserted just before the end (m. 92 in the score), and the bowing in this passage was changed to the upper marks given above. But only the original edition gives the authentic phrasing, unfortunately not to be found, for example, in the Peters edition. At mm. 182 ff. the Va. and D.B. were originally supplied with legato phrases.

In mm. 211 ff., the Bns. sounded an octave lower, and the notes for the Cls. and Bns. were:

[music notation: m. 211 Cls. / Bns.]

4. See below, p. 165. [*Editor*]

It is worth noting in mm. 222 ff. the violas retained the f♯ of the preceding measures; Beethoven changed it to d because in the meantime the F♯ of the D.B. had become the leading tone.

At m. 240 Beethoven's first plan was to have an arrangement similar to m. 228, with the first eighth on B in the D.B. *ff* (D.B. *only*, in an attempt to contrast with m. 228) ; all the other instruments (Vn., Va., and winds) entered on the second eighth, all *ff*. Because of the insertion of m. 240, the choric idea is first developed whereby on the first quarter the Vn. I, Vn. II, and Va. are marked merely *f*. Consequently, not only is the first edition incorrect in its reproduction of these two measures, since in m. 240 it gives the *ff* in the D.B. only on the second eighth (the first eighth is still *pp*) ; but also, for example, the Peters edition is incorrect, since it marks *f* the string chord at the beginning of m. 240, including the D.B.

At m. 303 the Vcs. were to have played with the Bns., another proof of how little Beethoven had thought specifically of the Hn. at this spot.

In mm. 323 ff., Vn. I originally had the melody to itself throughout (now it alternates with the winds) ; also, the Vc. was given its own voice-leading here:

Mm. 331 ff.: the bowing difficulties return as in the first section, mm. 86 ff.; also, Beethoven changes F to F♯ too soon (as early as the third repetition of the motive) so that the figure A–G–F♯ is repeated too often; besides this, a horn sound: $^{a\flat^1}_{f^1}$ is introduced.

In m. 386, the fifth measure of the group beginning at m. 382, a barline was inserted subsequently; thereby the original eight-measure group, the seventh measure of which was a general pause, becomes a nine-measure one, with the eighth measure empty and the ninth measure serving as an upbeat to the next group.

At mm. 400 ff. Beethoven had great difficulties to overcome in the passage for the horns. In mm. 407-11 the Vc. went along with the D.B. In mm. 429 ff. the bass was conceived throughout in half notes:

(one octave lower)

At m. 442 the Vns. sounded an octave higher. From a separate sheet we learn that the passage at mm. 469 ff. was originally set for strings only. At m. 500 Beethoven first thought of an extension of the close in powerful half notes, as follows:

(2 octaves lower)

then, on another sheet, he considered merely an alternation of chords on the tonic and dominant, until finally he threw out this version and contented himself with only two measures.

Here are the corrections for the errors that have remained in the published scores:

1. The slur beginning in m. 63 in the Vas. lasts for four measures: similarly in mm. 67-70, 71-74, and finally in the parallel passages of the recapitulation, mm. 307-10 and 315-18. Wherever a Va. figure contains a repetition of a pitch, however, as in mm. 75-78 or 79-82, two two-measure bows are correct. The first edition only partly restores these bowings.

2. The slur for the Bn. at m. 67 extends for four measures, thus mm. 67-70, 71-74, 75-78, and 79-82; likewise at the parallel places, mm. 311 ff. The first edition follows the autograph here almost throughout.

3. The crescendo in m. 83 for Cl., Bn., and Hn. must be omitted; it comes in m. 84, according to both autograph and first edition.

4. The slurs beginning in m. 88 for Vn. I and II extend for six measures! The first edition confirms this phrasing (see Ex. 9 in the Schenker analysis below, p. 175).

5. In m. 95 (also in m. 103^5 and in the parallel places, mm. 347 and 355) the staccato marks for Vn. I and II are to be deleted (the autograph and first edition have no marks).

6. In m. 439 the staccato marks in the strings and Timp. are to be deleted (the first edition is incorrect here).

SECOND MOVEMENT

In Nottebohm's *Beethoveniana*, I, 63, can be found some passages from the sketches for the second movement. Also to be considered from among the sketches are the first drafts and notes in the margins of the manuscript copy intended for the engraver, and—even more—those earlier versions of certain passages found in the body of the manuscript. Some have already been mentioned.[6] Here are some more:

Mm. 12-14 originally had thick voice leading, strongly permeated with motives.

In m. 28, the Hn. enters earlier, on the third eighth.

In m. 33, the first version for the Timp. was evidently the same as the first version in mm. 154-55: ♪ ♪ 𝄾 (see below).

In m. 37, along with the sign ══▶ , there is specifically added the

5. Schenker gives m. 102, evidently a typographical error. [*Editor*]
6. In Schenker's analysis of the second movement, omitted here. [*Editor*]

word "diminuendo."[7]

In m. 48 the Bns. were given an octave jump from the second to the third eighth note.

In mm. 57-58 the independent part for Bn. II was crossed out and a unison of both Bns. substituted.

In m. 80 a run of thirty-second notes from C to c was contemplated for the basses.

At the beginning of the second variation (m. 98) the Cl. (which is now silent) was to be given a figure with the rhythm [musical notation] .

In m. 107 the Vas. were to enter divisi; subsequently the double stops were divided between the Va. and Vc., but in a register that was lower than the final one. Furthermore, the original rhythm for Bn. and Cl. was different.

In m. 114 Vns. I and II originally had triple stops in eighth notes.

In m. 132 the countermelodies in the Cl. entered simultaneously with the imitative passage of the Ob.

In mm. 154-55 (cf. above, mm. 33 ff.) the Timp. had a rest in the third eighth.

In mm. 167 ff. the Vn. I had the melody (an octave below the Fl.), and Vn. II (in double stops) and Va. (in thirty-second-note arpeggios) accompanied. Finally, however, the corrections in mm. 172-77 became so extensive that Beethoven wrote out both pages again.

In m. 180 the D.B. originally entered on c, as does the Vn. in m. 179, and thereby reached the seventh (g) too early.

In mm. 187-88 and later in mm. 191-94, the Hn. and Timp. originally had the rhythm: [musical notation]

In mm. 191-94 the Fl., Cl., and Bn., by continuing their imitation of the main material, spoiled the overall effect of the music, chiefly because the first general climax is reached on the fifth degree (E♭), i.e. in m. 191 (cf. m. 7).

The errors that are to be found in the second movement in the printed score are as follows:

1. In mm. 23 and 25 (likewise in mm. 72 and 74), the slur in the winds should, according to the autograph, end on the third eighth (a purposeful contrast to the phrasing of Vn. I and II: the winds end the phrase on a quarter note, while the violins have only an eighth; this is already wrong in the first edition).

2. In m. 30 Beethoven starts the staccato marks on the thirty-second note (rather than on the dotted sixteenth) in all instruments, and with equal care does the same at m. 79. The first edition agrees with the autograph.

3. In mm. 35 and 36 the Timp. have the *sf* under the first quarter note. The misreading of the autograph, even in the first edition, obviously

7. Schenker earlier (in the analysis, omitted here) had shown how the autograph clearly indicates that in mm. 38–39 the cellos had originally been given the rhythm (together with Vn. II and Va.), but that Beethoven had changed it to make a rhythm in mm. 39–40 which would parallel that in mm. 27–28. [*Editor*]

originates from the fact that Beethoven, when correcting the original rhythm to a trill on the first quarter (see above) forgot, as so often happens, to move the *sf* along with it. In any case, an *sf* on the third eighth makes no sense.

4. In m. 40 Bn. II also has a tie. (For this should be leading directly into a state of suspended motion, so to speak, in which the dotted quarters progress in a seemingly unmeasured fashion; already wrong in the first edition.)

5. The e of Bn. II in m. 41 is likewise tied; see the Vc. (wrong in the first edition).

6. From mm. 41 to 47 (also in mm. 90 ff.) there should be a **legato slur for all instruments**, although Beethoven wrote this out only for the Vn. I, Vc., and Bn. II, and supplied only ties for the inner voices; evidently he calculated that the legato phrasing for the outer voices would be understood as applying to the others. (The first edition introduces the slur arbitrarily.)

7. The f$\sharp^2$ and the g^2 for Cl. in mm. 53 and 54 are not slurred; this is confirmed in the manuscript and also in the parallel place, mm. 102-03, where the E-F for Fl., Ob., and Bn. are also not to be played legato. (In the first edition only the latter case is correct.)

N.B. In m. 55, the first edition, contrary to the manuscript, has a slur for the Cl. (The full score, which has no slur, is correct.)

8. In mm. 57-59, Bn. II plays with Bn. I. (The first edition probably overlooked Beethoven's *unisono* indication.)

9. In m. 57, a lower voice of three sixteenth notes is to be added to the last three sixteenth notes of the Va. The notes clearly were inserted in the autograph later; also, however, in mm. 8-10 this lower voice (e♭) in the Va. appears, from the difference of the handwriting, to have been added later. (In the first edition this lower voice is overlooked.)

10. In m. 97 an *ff* is marked only for the octave jumps by the Va. and Bn., as opposed to an *f* for the octave jump of the Vc. and Cl. Also the sixteenth note e♭^{2} of the Ob. and Fl. should be marked *f*, not *ff*. (The fact that Beethoven put a second *f* on the downbeat of the following measures for these instruments—also given in the first edition—caused the later engravers and correctors to arbitrarily put an *ff* at m. 97, instead of two *f*'s, separated from one another by a barline.

N.B. In m. 104 in the autograph, there is a legato slur for the Fl. but not for the Ob. and Bsn.; however, to correspond with m. 55 this legato marking should be rejected.

11. In mm. 132, 133, 134, and 135, the slur ends on the last sixteenth (cf. mm. 128 and 130); the same articulation applies then to the Ob. and later the Cl. (wrong in the first edition).

12. All the sixteenth notes of the Cl. in mm. 136-37 fall under one slur (incorrect in the first edition).

13. The new slur for the Cl. stops at the end of m. 138.

14. The same applies to m. 139.

15. The second slur for the Fl. and Ob. in m. 137 ends with the last sixteenth note, also the slur in m. 139.

16. In m. 142 the $\diagup\!\!\!\diagup$ should stop on the third sixteenth. (In

the first edition, our items 13-16 are incorrect.)

17. In mm. 194-95, the Cl. II makes an ascending leap of a tenth, d¹–f², exactly like the Bn. II (correct in the first edition) .

18. Across the barline between mm. 216-17, the Hns. play g¹–c¹, exactly as between mm. 214 and 215 (the g¹ is already missing in the first edition) .

19. In m. 217 the Bn. should have a *p* before the *cresc.*, and the D.B. a *cresc.* on the last sixteenth notes.

20. In m. 218 Bn. I should hold e♭¹ for a quarter note, which is then tied through m. 219! Thus the extension intended here (of the passage earlier encountered at mm. 11, 60, and 195) is made clear. But this requires further that the sign ⟍ for Fl. I, Cl. II, and Bn. I already begins on the third eighth note of m. 218.

21. In mm. 224-25, both Bns. do not sound until the last sixteenth note! The first version of mm. 225-26 needed so much rewriting that Beethoven wrote this passage out again to make it clear; there he specifically indicated at m. 225 the rests ⅞ ⅞⋅ before the last sixteenth note, but forgot to strike out the Bn. part for m. 224 (cf. the *sf* for Timp. in mm. 35-36) . In reality, as emerges from the instrumental layout of mm. 224-28, the winds participate starting with the last sixteenth note of m. 225, and continue through m. 226. (The first edition faithfully reproduces the part left in by mistake.)

22. In m. 225, the last sixteenth note of the D.B. should be slurred to the first eighth note of m. 226.

23. In m. 226, there is a slur in the D.B. between b and c¹.

24. In m. 230, the slurs for Cl. and Bn. end with the barline.

25. The same is true with the slurs for Vn. I and Vn. II at mm. 232, 233, and 234; only with the Va. in mm. 235 ff. does the slur include all three notes.

THIRD MOVEMENT

I would like to show one of the sketches preserved in the archives of the Gesellschaft der Musikfreunde in Vienna, which Nottebohm has not published; it contains drafts of the bass line for m. 124 ff.:

Here one can see the composer wrestling with the problem of the delayed arpeggiation. The first line shows no less than three full cadences with I-IV-V-I, the second—longer by a couple of measures—has two cadences, the third is a step backwards, and the fourth elaborates the IV degree.

Now to the sketches found in the manuscript:

From mm. 24 to 25, the passing note, B♭, is missing in the bass; its insertion prepares the horn's descent in mm. 25-26.

In mm. 27 ff., the Hn. originally had the Bn. part, and vice versa; the correction gives the horn a more suitable continuation of its soloistic material in mm. 19-26.

It is worth mentioning that in mm. 38 and 40 of the Bn. part, the slurs originally connected the half note and the quarter on the third beat—by which means Beethoven perhaps had originally sought consistency with the slurring of the other instruments in mm. 39 and 41; but in the Cl. part (with the same figure an octave higher) he had already tied the third quarter of m. 38 to the dotted half of m. 39; similarly in the parallel places, mm. 90 and 92. In point of fact this consistency mentioned above was not well-grounded, since the Bn. and Cl. cut through with their *sf* on the third quarter, while all the other instruments had it placed at the beginning of the two measures.

In mm. 49-50, Vn. I was reinforced by Fl. I, and the descent in thirds of Vn. II and Va. by both Cls.

Among the many corrections observable at mm. 109 ff., only the following will be mentioned: Fl. and Ob. had already entered in m. 109; Timp. entered in m. 110; in mm. 115 ff., the Timp. (now silent) were given the rhythm of the winds, *sempre pp.*

In mm. 153-54, the Bn. continued to double the D.B.

The shaping of the counterpoint in mm. 154 ff. in Vn. II, and Va. presented difficulties. In m. 157, Vn. II rather than Va. moved in sixths with Vn. I.

In mm. 170 ff., the counterpoint of the basses was syncopated, and the syncopation continued through the passage comprising mm. 174-77 and also to mm. 178 ff. However, from m. 182 on, the bass on G is inverted, i.e., with octave register reversed.

In mm. 184 ff., the manuscript shows an attempt to use the main motive of the trio as counterpoint in Vn. I (this motive having been used in the top notes of the Fl. at mm. 182-83 and having, in general, permeated the orchestral fabric).

In m. 267 the Bn. originally had g, and in m. 271 e♭.

In mm. 285 ff., the Vc. had rests on the 2nd and 3rd quarter notes.

In mm. 295-96, and also in mm. 297-98, the Va. had responded in reversed order—with the notes f^1 and $a♭^1$—to the notes $a♭^2$ and f^2 of Vn. I.

In mm. 300 ff., Vn. II did not yet have a rest on the first quarter.

Also in mm. 318 ff., the Bn. still had the bass line. What a happy correction to put the bassoon on its own just before the deceptive cadence!

Clearly in order to prepare the *cresc.*, but above all to prepare the four-measure group (which it is now left only to the Timp. to preserve), the bassoon had already entered at m. 336 with $\frac{c}{c^1}$.

In mm. 339 ff., the bass proceeded in dotted halves; from m. 350 on, however, it remained on G.

Vn. II accompanied the rising motion of Vn. I (in which the descending sixth is elaborated) in such a way as to give greater weight to the lower note of these sixths. Vn. II even displaced these notes; for example, b^1 has already been sounded on the third quarter of m. 359. The Va., however, followed Vn. I, mainly in sixths. Overall, one observes a difficult struggle on the composer's part to devise a contrapuntal accompaniment for the melody of Vn. I, the shaping of which had already caused him much trouble. Finally he had to leave it to Vn. I to state the sixths alone and unobtrusively, without the assistance of other instruments.

The Ob. had already entered in m. 366 with $^{f2}_{a1}$, and in m. 367 Vn. II sounded an octave lower.

Here is a list of the points misrepresented by the printed scores:

1. In m. 13, the D.B. should have *sf* >— (this in the autograph; in the first edition there is an *sfp*.)

2. In m. 14 the slur in the D.B. should start with the downbeat half note (correct in the first edition).

3. In m. 56, the slur in the D.B. starts on f.

4. In m. 60, a new slur begins for Va. (It prepares for the phrasing of the lower strings in the following measures; correct in the first edition).

N.B. In mm. 76 and 84 Beethoven does not put slurs in the D.B., although he has supplied them in mm. 32 and 36 (the first edition follows the manuscript); doubtless the non-legato is influenced by the heavy dotted halves in mm. 71-75 (as opposed to the quarters of mm. 20-23) and also by the *ff* [in the other instruments] from mm. 79 ff. and mm. 83 ff.

5. In m. 96 the Tpt. has a *p* without anything added (in the manuscript the original *dimin.* is crossed out and a *piano* clearly inserted; but already by the first edition there is *p, dim. pp,* clearly to bring the dynamic marking of the Tpt. into conformity with the other instruments).

N.B. In m. 101 the Vc. lacks any dynamic marks (also in the first edition), yet in view of the autograph marking of *f* >— *p* in mm. 105 and 109 (which in the first edition is merely *fp*) a *p* should be understood, rather than the *pp* of m. 97.

6. In m. 110 the Va. has a *p* added (in both autograph and first edition).

7. The slur that starts at m. 114 in the Vc. continues uninterrupted until m. 130; this applies also to the bassoon! (Although the manuscript leaves no doubt about this, the slur is already divided in the first edition.)

8. At m. 154 (according to both the autograph and the first edition) there should be an *ff* at the entrance of the 1st Vn.

9. Similarly, at m. 157, there is an *ff* for the 1st Fl.

10. From m. 255 on, the mark *sempre pp* refers only to those instruments which have the arpeggiated grace notes—thus 1st Vn. in m. 255, Va. in mm. 259, 270, and 289 (according to the autograph).

11. In m. 255 the Vc. has a *p* instead of *pp* (according to both autograph and first edition).

12. Similarly, in m. 267, only one *p* for the Bn.

13. In m. 295, the horn should have *pp* (thus in the autograph; the first edition has *p*).

14. In m. 360 a new slur starts for the 1st Vn. and continues until m. 366. (The first edition breaks it, against the clear wishes of the composer.)

FOURTH MOVEMENT

Here are some noteworthy details from the composer's finishing touches in the autograph:

In mm. 1-6 the Alto and Tenor Trb. lines lay higher; true also of the Va. in mm. 4-5.

In mm. 20-21 the motion $\frac{5\text{-}6}{3\text{-}4}$ occurred on the quarter notes.

In mm. 30-31 the Fl. played along with the other melody instruments.

In mm. 34-37 Bn. I and Va. helped fill the spaces with a motive of their own, in the rhythm: ♪♪♪♪ ♪♪ ♩

In m. 45 the accompanying triplet figure of the 2nd Vn. and Va. remained on only one pitch.

In mm. 46 ff. the Va. joined the Vc. (as later in the development, mm. 91 ff.).

In mm. 51 ff. starting with the quarter-note upbeat, the Bn. took part in the string texture; in addition, the 1st Bn. was used to connect mm. 51 and 52; this was repeated beginning with the 4th beat of m. 52.

In m. 61 the Ob. originally joined the Fl. in its sixteenth notes.

The composer had great difficulty arriving at the final instrumentation for the closing theme; first and foremost the corrections show that the original idea here was to give the theme to the Cl. alone and not the Va.; the Cls. were marked *unisono*, while the Va. (in m. 64!) turned from g^1 to $d\sharp^1$ (now in Vn. II).

In m. 96 the Va. carried out a progression, interrupted by rests on the 1st and 3rd quarters, in contrary motion to the Vc., cf. mm. 295 ff. in the transition of the coda. After the composer had crossed out this counterpoint, he gave this countermaterial over to the Ob. and Fl., by which the passage for winds, mm. 99 ff., is most happily introduced. This latter passage evidently was originally intended for strings.

From the 4th quarter of m. 118 on, the Timp. on G was also used.

In mm. 120-22 the Vc. (like the D.B.) remained on C.

In mm. 175-91 Vn. I joined the Ob.

Just before the recapitulation, the Timp. entered at m. 200, (at first, to be sure, with only three quarter-note beats per bar); Vn. I entered with b^2 as early as m. 203.

In m. 254 Vn. II played the same accompaniment as in m. 45.

Again in the closing theme of the recapitulation, mm. 273 ff., there were the same intensive searches for the correct instrumentation as in the first part.

The sixteenth-note figures of Vn. I in mm. 274-77 lay an octave higher.

In mm. 303 ff. a polyphonic elaboration was attempted—that is, a developing in independent figures by both Vn. I and Va.

In mm. 317-19 of the coda, the Hn. doubled the Bn., as in the repetition later at mm. 335 ff.; and in mm. 319-21 Vn. I, Va., and Vc. doubled the Hn; moreover, Vn. I at first played the motive that the Fl. has now.

In mm. 329-32 the Va. joined with the D.B.

On the way to the *stretta* at mm. 350 ff. the Hns. also assisted [in the bass line].

Beginning at m. 404 Vn. I held on the high c³ throughout; with the levelling-down and the arpeggio e²–g²–c³ in mm. 414-16 the first impatience to close was allayed. Again with the c³ in m. 416 the composer made an attempt to close; he also overcame this and went on finally to the third and last rise at m. 428.

To be noted in the printed scores:

1. In m. 6 the last three eighths are for Bn. I only (according to the autograph; the first edition says *unisono*.)

2. In mm. 34-35 the slurs for Vn. I and Vn. II extend over both measures; the same goes for mm. 36-37, as well as the parallel places, mm. 240 ff. (The first edition, which doesn't agree with the manuscript concerning the slurs for the melody in the winds in mm. 26-27 and mm. 30-31, is in agreement from mm. 34 ff.)

N.B. In mm. 38-40 the manuscript shows different slurs for Bn. I than Va., even though they have the same notes: for the Bn. a whole measure slur, for the Va. only a half (upbow); the slurs do agree in the parallel place, mm. 247-49 (for the Fl., Ob., and Bn. who have the same line). The first edition eliminates the discrepancy in mm. 38-40 and gives the Bn. the same slur as the Va.

3. In mm. 51 and 53 the slur for Vns. I and II only goes to the end of the measure.

4. In mm. 64-65, 66-67, and 68-69, the slurs for the Cl. and Va., which have the theme, and for Bn. II, which has parallel sixths below, start on the fourth quarter. Bn. I plays both half notes in mm. 64, 66, and 68 *non legato*; it plays *legato* only the 1st and 2nd quarters of mm. 65, 67, and 69. The slur for Vn. I in mm. 65, 67, 69, 70, and 71 stops on the last sixteenth. Finally, the slur for Va. in m. 70 has already begun on the first half. (So Beethoven writes throughout in both the first part and the recapitulation, with the single exception of mm. 64-65, where he starts the slur for the Cl. on the dotted half. This particular slur pattern was taken by the first edition as a model for all equivalent places; furthermore that edition omits articulations for many instruments and gives wrong slurs for the violin figures. The articulation that Beethoven gives to the descent of the fourth enhances the *fp* effect as follows: during the sound of the first dotted half a new half note is struck on the upbeat by other instruments; this in itself then effects, even if in an artificial way, a kind of slurring of the sound.) The *sf* in Vn. I is to be eliminated in m. 68.

5. In m. 106 there should be a *stacc.* mark on the last quarter, B♮, of the bass instruments (D.B., Vc., Cbn.).

6. The same in m. 109 on the quarter-note c (the *stacc.* is already missing in the first edition.)

7. In mm. 118-19 the D♮s for both D.B. and Vc. are tied!

8. In m. 200 a new slur should begin on the F in Fl., Ob., and Bn. (in the first edition all slurs are missing from mm. 184 ff.).

9. In mm. 244-45 and 246-47 the slurs for the Va., unlike the D.B., span both measures. (Thus in the manuscript; the first edition makes the slurs for the D.B. conform with those for the Va.)

10. In mm. 296, 298, 300, and 302, the Hn., Tpt. and Timp. have *sf* instead of *f*!

N.B. In mm. 322 ff., according to the manuscript, the phrasing for Va. and Vc. is different; nevertheless the articulation of the Va. is valid for the Vc. (as in the first edition) when one considers that all these differences are mainly for the purpose of expressing a *legato*. The same goes for the repetition in mm. 339 ff. (Here again the first edition has indicated the bowing differently.)

ANALYSIS

Unless specified otherwise, all numbered footnotes in the following essays are those of the author. References in the essays to notebooks, letters, and other essays reprinted in the Norton Critical Score have been bracketed and changed to refer to this edition.

DONALD FRANCIS TOVEY

[The Fifth Symphony]†

Sir Donald Francis Tovey (1875-1940), English musician, is best known for his lucid essays on music, but he was also active as a composer and pianist. In 1914 he became Reid Professor of Music at Edinburgh, where he organised the Reid Symphony Orchestra. His six volumes of *Essays in Musical Analysis*, organised by genre, cover a wide range of literature. His essay on the Fifth Symphony was the first account in English to be concerned with this music primarily as sound. Graced by Tovey's wit, it remains a classic of its kind.

This work shares with Beethoven's Seventh Symphony the distinction of being not only among the most popular but also among the least misunderstood of musical classics. It has not failed to inspire "roaring cataracts of nonsense" from commentators, but the nonsense has, for the most part, been confined to technical matters of little concern to the naïve (or ideal) listener; though one heresy I shall discuss here, since on it depends one's whole view of the difference between real composition and mere manufacture. Another immensely lucky fact conducive to the popular appreciation of this symphony is that the famous phrase (made still more famous by Robert Louis Stevenson in *The Ebb Tide*) —the phrase which describes the theme of the first movement as "destiny knocking at the door"—is no mere figment of a commentator, but is Beethoven's very own words. Mistakes and misreadings in this mighty work have been as frequent as anywhere; the very band-parts issued under the auspices of the "critical" edition have some scandalously stupid editorial alterations; but not even the notorious old trick of changing the first three quavers into crotchets [i.e. quarter note] has been able to make any headway against the overwhelming power and clearness of the whole.

Some good, however, may be done by denouncing the heresy which preaches that "the whole first movement is built up of the initial figure

† From *Essays in Musical Analysis*, London, 1935, I, 38–44. Published by Oxford University Press; reprinted by permission.

of four notes". It is well worth refuting, for it has led to most of the worst features of that kind of academic music which goes furthest to justify the use of the word "academic" as a term of vulgar abuse. No great music has ever been built from an initial figure of four notes. As I have said elsewhere, you might as well say that every piece of music is built from an initial figure of *one* note. You may profitably say that the highest living creatures have begun from the single nucleated cell. But no ultra-microscope has yet unravelled the complexities of the single living cell; nor, if the spectroscope is to be believed, are we yet very fully informed of the complexities of a single atom of iron: and it is quite absurd to suppose that the evolution of a piece of music can proceed from "a simple figure of four notes" on lines in the least resembling those of nature. As far as I know, Weingartner[1] is the first writer who has pointed out the truth that the first movement of the C minor symphony is really remarkable for the length of its sentences; that the first sentences, instead of being "built up" from a single figure, *break up* into other sentences of even greater variety and breadth; and that the composer who first really "built up" symphonic movements out of short figures was not Beethoven but Schumann, whose handling of the larger forms became sectional, diffuse, and yet stiff for this very reason.

Obviously the same argument applies to the whole theory of Wagnerian *Leitmotif*. Wagner attained full mastery over the broadest sweep of sequence that music has yet achieved. This alone suffices to refute the orthodox Wagnerian belief that his music is "built up" from the scraps of theme to which it can be reduced by its dramatic associations, and by the general possibility of articulating big phrases into small figures.

In the first fine careless rapture of Wagnerian analysis it was discovered that the "four taps", with which "destiny knocks at the door" in the first movement, recur elsewhere; once (quite accidentally, though in an impressive passage) in the slow movement, and very prominently in the second theme of that dream of terror which we technically call the scherzo (Ex. 4). This profound discovery was supposed to reveal an unsuspected unity in the work; but it does not seem to have been carried far enough. It conclusively proves that the Sonata Appassionata, the G major Pianoforte Concerto, the third movement of the Quartet, op. 74, and, with the final consummation of a fifth tap, the Violin Concerto, all belong to the C minor Symphony; for the same rhythmic figure pervades them too. The simple truth is that Beethoven could not do without just such purely rhythmic figures at this stage of his art. It was absolutely

1. Felix Weingartner, *The Symphony Since Beethoven*, transl. H. M. Schott, New York, 1969, p. 259. Weingartner's book was first published in 1898. [*Editor*]

necessary that every inner part in his texture should assert its own life; but at the same time it was equally necessary that it should not cause constant or rapid changes of harmony by doing so. Figures that can identify a theme while remaining on one note are the natural response to these requirements. In his later works Beethoven used more and more polyphony in Bach's sense; and rhythmic figures no longer pressed into the foreground of his invention, though he could still use them when he wanted them. It is astonishing how many of Beethoven's themes can be recognized by their bare rhythm without quoting any melody at all.

Here are some specimens, not including those mentioned above:

In selecting the following illustrations for the C minor Symphony I have been guided mainly by the purpose of counteracting the effects of the "short figure" heresy, and secondly, by the chance of removing by numerals a misconception which is likely to arise from the notation of long sentences in such very short bars. Thus Ex. 1 evidently comprises

Ex. 1

only the first half of a big sentence. (The crotchet tails and the small added notes show the pathetic new light in which it appears at the very end of the movement.)

Ex. 2, which gives the opening of the second subject, shows first the way in which the famous rhythmic figure (*a*) pervades the whole movement, and secondly, with the aid of my numerals, the scansion of the four-bar rhythm.

Ex. 2

From the second and third bars of this quotation (marked 1 and 2 in the rhythmic periods) are derived, first, the famous diminuendo of chords in dialogue between strings and wind near the end of the development, and secondly, the furious opening of the coda, one of the most powerful tuttis ever written, and written with incredibly few notes for its weight. Of the recapitulation two observations may here be made: first, that, as Weingartner points out, the pathetic cadenza for the oboe at the end of Ex. 1 is the outcome of a melodic line which it has been tracing for the last sixteen bars; and secondly, that it is really a mistaken reverence for Beethoven which puts up with the comic bassoon instead of horns when we have Ex. 2 in C major. Beethoven had not time to change the horns from E flat; but now that the modern horn has all the notes that were missing in Beethoven's day, there is no reason why his spirit should continue to put up with an unmitigated nuisance, even if we are sure that he put up with it in a mood of Shakespearian humor. The continuation of the passage has a bitter note that was not in the original statement.

The andante I have left without illustration. Shakespeare's women have the same courage, the same beauty of goodness, and the same humour. In form the movement is unique, if dimly suggested by Haydn's special form of variations on two alternating themes. But here the themes are of quite peculiar types. Violas and cellos (it is curious that Beethoven never uses orchestral cellos for melody without doubling them by violas) state the first theme in a single broad phrase, the end of which the higher instruments echo and carry on into a series of echoing afterthoughts. Then the second theme begins, very simply, pauses on a wistful note, and suddenly bursts into a blaze of triumph in a remote key, C major, the tonic of the whole symphony. The triumph dies away into a passage of profound mystery and pathos, which leads back to the key of the movement (A flat). The first theme now returns varied in notes twice as rapid as the time-beats (the kind of variation which in the eighteenth century would be called a double). A clarinet holds a sustained note above, with a boldness which led critics to suspect a blunder. (Dvořák did not think so when he reproduced it in the slow movement of his first symphony). Again the second theme follows, likewise with a quicker accompaniment, and leads to its blaze of triumph, which again dies out in the recognition that its day is not yet come. A second double of the first theme follows in due course, but, instead of getting beyond the first phrase, is given three times, the last time forte, leading to a climax and a pause. Then there is an astonishing series of mediations and adventures, on which the second theme breaks with its full note of triumph. The reaction from this (in one of those profound passages which early critics found quite ridiculous because they listened with ears attuned to the proportions of a Mozart symphony) leads to an exquisite treatment of the first theme smiling through tears in the minor mode. Then, after more meditative delay, it comes fortissimo, for the first and only time, on the full orchestra. Note the imitation by the wood-wind, if you can hear it through the far from evenly-balanced scoring. This time the echoing afterthoughts follow; and nothing in music is bolder and more convincing than the profusion with which these afterthoughts give rise to others, until the whole movement is rounded off in perfect proportions which at no point have revealed to us what they are going to be until the last note has been heard.

The third movement I will not describe seriatim; but there is one piece of information which is very interesting historically, and which commentators, including Sir George Grove, have failed to make as clear as it might be. My quotations are again furnished with numerals which show where the pulses of four-bar rhythm begin. The movement has often been scanned wrongly from beginning to end, and the writer in *Grove's Dictionary* who cites the trio as an unacknowledged case of three-bar rhythm has blundered straight into the trap.

Ex. 3

Ex. 4

Now it is well known that in the early editions there were two super-fluous bars where the first theme (Ex. 3) returns after the trio. The second and third full bars (marked 1 and 2 in my rhythmic numbers) were written twice, at first legato as in Ex. 3, and then in crotchets with rests, as they ought to be after the trio. Beethoven wrote to his publishers to correct the redundancy; but it still remained upheld as a stroke of genius forty years after his death.

How did it originate? The answer is that this movement was, until after its first performance, meant to be of the same form as the scherzos of the Fourth, Sixth, and Seventh Symphonies (compare also the Piano-forte Trios, op. 70, no. 2, and op. 97, and the String Quartets, op. 59, no. 2, opp. 74, 95, and 132) —that is to say, the whole movement, trio and all, was to be given twice; and the breathless pianissimo da capo was to be the third presentation of the main theme. The redundant bars were for the *prima volta*, and they led back to bar four of Ex. 3 (here marked 3 in my rhythmic periods). The double-bar and 𝄋 that must have stood there at the time would have had the effect of making it impossible to misread the rhythm; and Beethoven had actually chosen this point for marking his repeat, though it forced him to write out those two bars which afterwards became redundant when the repeat was abandoned. That it was abandoned shows how Beethoven's own special form of the round-and-round scherzo, alternating twice over with its trio, had to yield to the terrific impressiveness of the emotions created by these themes. Probably the long repeat proved detrimental, not to the great darkness that leads to the finale (nothing could weaken that), but to the reap-pearance of the "scherzo" in the development of the finale.

In the finale trombones appear for the first time in symphonic music. I quote a part of the first theme in order to show that it is again a

Ex. 6

case of a magnificently long sentence, weighted with repetitions even more powerful than those of the first movement, inasmuch as they are not sequential repetitions, but plain reiterations on the same position in the scale.

The main theme of the second subject (Ex. 7) I quote in order to point out that the minims [i.e. half notes] in the cellos form an important figure (c) turned to powerful account in the development.

Ex. 7

The final theme of the second subject (Ex. 8) is destined to be worked up in the presto coda.

Ex. 8

Spohr,[2] who thought the theme of the first movement scrappy and undignified, and the whole finale an orgy of vulgar noise, admitted that the reappearance of the "scherzo" in the middle of the finale was a stroke of genius for which the rest of the work might be forgiven. It is indeed a stroke of genius. Spohr liked it because it was interesting as a feature of form. He evidently disbelieved or disapproved of anything that could be said about emotional values in this symphony, and so he can hardly have realized where the genius really lay in the stroke. Let us remember that the "scherzo" had a tremendous emotional value, and then consider how it is to be reintroduced into the sustained triumph of the finale. Any one would think that there were only two ways of working the problem: first, to reproduce the mood just as it was. Of course this is impossible. We cannot forget that the terror is passed. Secondly then, could we recover the mood by elaborating the details? This would betray itself as fictitious. If you cannot recover the sensations you felt during an earthquake, it is not much use telling as your own experience things about it that you could not possibly have known at the time. We can easily see, now that Beethoven has shown us, that his is the one true solution which confirms the truth of the former terror and the security of the present triumph; but no lesser artist could have found it. Beethoven recalls the third movement as a memory which we know for a fact but can no longer under-

2. See below, p. 186. [*Editor*]

stand: there is now a note of self-pity, for which we had no leisure when the terror was upon our souls: the depth and the darkness are alike absent, and in the dry light of day we cannot remember our fears of the unknown. And so the triumph resumes its progress and enlarges its range until it reaches its appointed end.

E. T. A. HOFFMANN

[*Review of the Fifth Symphony*]†

E. T. A. Hoffmann (1776-1822) was the first critic to give a serious review in depth not only to Beethoven's music but to any important music in the nineteenth century. He has been called the father of modern musical criticism and not without reason. In turn a composer, music teacher, and musical director in his early life, during which time his formal studies were in jurisprudence, he became increasingly attracted in his thirties to a career in writing. From 1809 to 1815 he was associated with the Leipzig publishers Breitkopf & Härtel and their journal, the *Allgemeine musikalische Zeitung*. Under the editorship of Johann Friedrich Rochlitz, this house organ became the leading musical journal in Europe, a position due primarily to the editor's choice of contributors, of whom Hoffmann was the most gifted. Hoffmann's review of the Fifth Symphony introduced a new concept of artistic criticism, whereby the artist saw this kind of writing as a logical extension of his creative endeavors, as a means of expressing his views concerning not only the art work in question but also musical art in general and its relation to the other arts. Later composers, especially Berlioz, Schumann, and Wagner, were to follow in his path.

The reviewer has before him one of the most important works of the master whose stature as a first-rate instrumental composer probably no one will now dispute. He is profoundly moved by the object he is to discuss; no one can reproach him for stepping beyond the usual bounds of criticism and striving to capture in words the feelings this composition

† From *Allgemeine musikalische Zeitung*, XII/40, 41 (July 4 and 11, 1810), 630–42 and 652–59. Most of Hoffmann's examples have been replaced by references to the score. The translation is by F. John Adams, Jr. Portions of a later version of this essay are reprinted in Oliver Strunk, ed., *Source Readings in Music History*, New York, 1950, pp. 775–81.

aroused deep within his heart.

If one speaks of music as an independent art, one should always have instrumental music in mind. Only instrumental music, which scorns all assistance from and combination with other art, can express with purity music's peculiar nature. It alone can give definition to the art. Music is the most romantic of all the arts; one might even say that it alone is purely romantic. The lyre of Orpheus opened the gates of Orcus. Music unlocks for man an unfamiliar world having nothing in common with the external material world which surrounds him. It is a world where he forgets all feelings which he could define for another in order to surrender himself to the inexpressible. How little the peculiar nature of music was recognized by the instrumental composers who tried to represent definable feelings or even events through their music and thus attempted to treat their art, which stands in direct opposition to plastic art, in a plastic way! The Dittersdorf symphonies of this type[1], together with all the recent *Batailles des trois Empereurs* etc.[2], are ludicrous aberrations which ought to be punished by burial in oblivion. In song, where the words of the accompanying poetry suggest definite effects, it is the music which acts as the sage's miracle elixir, a few drops of which make every drink both precious and exquisite. Every passion— love, hate, anger, despair—as opera reveals them to us, is clothed by music in the radiant purple of romanticism; precisely that which we have felt in life leads us out from life into the realm of the infinite. The magic of music is so strong! Always having the stronger effect, this magic must tear to pieces any fetters imposed on it by another art.

Certainly it is not solely to improvements in the means of musical expression (perfection of instruments, greater virtuosity in the performers) that one should look to understand how gifted composers have been able to lift instrumental music to its present height. This phenomenon has arisen also from a more profound, a more intimate recognition of the peculiar nature of music. Haydn and Mozart, the creators of modern instrumental music, were the first to show us the art in its full glory. It is Beethoven who regarded that art with an ardent love and penetrated

1. In the list of symphonies by Dittersdorf in MGG (III, 594), the following contain descriptive titles: *Sinfonia nel gusto di cinque nazioni*, in A (1767); *Trois Simphonies exprimant trois métamorphoses d'Ovide: Les quatre âges du monde; La chûte de Phaéton; Actéon changé en cerf* (1785); plus the following undated symphonies based on the *Metamorphoses: Andromède sauvée par Persée; Phinée avec ses amis changés en rochers; Les paysans changés en grenouilles. [Editor]*

2. Oliver Strunk, *op. cit.*, p. 776n., suggests: "Perhaps Hoffmann is thinking of Louis Jadin's 'La grande bataille d'Austerlitz', published in an arrangement for the piano by Kühnel of Leipzig in 1807 or earlier." [*Editor*]

into its innermost essence. The instrumental compositions of all three masters breathe the same romantic spirit which, to be sure, grows out of the same intimate understanding of the peculiar nature of the art. The character of their compositions, however, is noticeably different.

The expression of a cheerful, childlike disposition can be found everywhere in the compositions of Haydn. His symphonies lead us into a boundless, green glade amid a lively, jovial throng of happy people. Young men and women swing past in round-dances, and laughing children, eavesdropping behind trees and rose bushes, throw flowers teasingly at one another. It is a life full of love and full of happiness, as if before sin—a life of eternal youth. There is no suffering, no pain, but only the sweet, melancholy longing for the beloved form which hovers far off in the evening's red glow, neither coming closer nor disappearing. As long as the form remains, night will not fall, for the form itself is the red of the evening which causes the mountain and glade to glow.

Mozart leads us into the inner depths of the realm of the spirits. Fear envelops us but does not torment us: it is more a premonition of the infinite. Love and melancholy sound forth with beautiful voices; night[3] falls in the world of the spirits amid the bright splendor of shimmering purple. We move with indescribable longing toward the forms which beckon us in a friendly way to their ranks to soar through the clouds in the eternal dance of the spheres (for example. Mozart's Symphony in E♭ major [i.e. No. 39] known as the "Swan Song") .

So also does the instrumental music of Beethoven open the realm of the colossal and the immeasurable for us. Radiant beams shoot through the deep night of this region, and we become aware of gigantic shadows which, rocking back and forth, close in on us and destroy all within us except the pain of endless longing—a longing in which every pleasure that rose up amid jubilant tones sinks and succumbs. Only through this pain, which, while consuming but not destroying love, hope, and joy, tries to burst our breasts with a full-voiced general cry from all the passions, do we live on and are captivated beholders of the spirits.

One seldom finds a person with romantic taste; romantic talent is even rarer. This is probably the reason why there are so few who can play that lyre which unlocks the marvelous realm of the infinite. Haydn has a romantic conception of the human in human life; he is more suitable for the majority. Mozart claims the superhuman, the amazing which dwells in the inner spirit. Beethoven's music induces terror, fright, horror and pain and awakens that endless longing which is the essence of

3. German is "Macht"; undoubtedly "Nacht" is intended. [Editor]

romanticism. Beethoven is a purely romantic composer (and precisely for this reason, a truly musical composer). Thus it may be that he is less successful with vocal music, since it does not admit indefinite longing but represents, from among the emotions that may be experienced in the realm of the infinite, only those which can be specified by words. The thoroughly romantic nature of his instrumental music may be the reason that it seldom receives the acclaim of the multitude. Even this multitude, however, which does not appreciate the profundity of Beethoven, does not deny him an active imagination. On the contrary, one usually views his works as products of a genius who, unconcerned with form and the selection of ideas, surrenders himself to his ardent passion and to the spontaneous inspiration of his powers of imagination. Nevertheless, he can be placed directly beside Haydn and Mozart with regard to his self-possession. He separates his "I" from the inner realm of the tones and commands it as an unrestricted lord. Just as the esthetic surveyors have often complained of a complete lack of true unity and inner coherence in Shakespeare, while only those of deeper vision have witnessed the springing forth of a beautiful tree, buds and leaves, blossoms and fruits, from a germinal seed—so too will only a very deep penetration into the inner structure of Beethoven's music reveal the great extent of the master's self-possession. Such self-possession is inseparable from true genius and is nourished by continuous study of the art. Deep within Beethoven's heart dwells the romanticism of his music—a romanticism which he reveals with great ingenuity and extreme care in his works. Never has the reviewer felt this more strongly than in the symphony presently before him. As it grows toward a climax at the end, this symphony unfolds Beethoven's romanticism more than any of his other works and tears the listener irresistibly away into the wonderful spiritual realm of the infinite.

The first Allegro,[4] in C minor and 2/4 meter, begins with the principal motive, which is stated completely in the first two measures and reappears again and again in many forms throughout the movement. In the second measure there is a fermata. A repetition of the principal motive follows, this time a step lower, again with a fermata. Both times only strings and clarinets have played. The key is still not well defined: the listener presumes E♭ major. Then the second violin restates the principal motive which is subsequently imitated by the viola and the first violin. The C-minor tonality is established in the second measure of this new section by the bass tone C which is played by the cellos and the bassoons. We are finally led from the principal motive to a two-measure passage

4. Beethoven specifies "Allegro con brio." [*Editor*]

which, repeated three times (the full orchestra entering for the last repetition), ends with a fermata on the dominant. A presentiment of the unknown, of the mysterious, is instilled in the listener. The beginning of the Allegro up to this pause determines the character of the entire piece. Precisely for this reason, the reviewer has inserted the whole passage here for the reader to see: [Hoffmann's example consists of the first 21 measures of the full score].

After this fermata the violins and the viola, remaining in the tonic, have the principal motive in imitation while the bass now and then plays a figure which echoes it. Then a transition passage builds in intensity, and once again the presentiment previously mentioned is aroused, this time more strongly and persistently than before. The transition passage leads to a tutti whose theme makes use of the rhythm of the principal motive to which it is intimately related: [mm. 44–48, first violins]. The $\frac{6}{3}$ chord built on D prepares the related key of E♭ major, in which the principal motive is once again stated, this time in a paraphrase by the horn. The first violin introduces a second theme which is certainly melodious but which still retains the character of anxious, restless longing asserted throughout the movement. This theme is carried alternately by the violins and clarinets. Every third measure the bass plays its previously mentioned echo of the principal motive, once again weaving the first theme into the artful fabric of the whole. As the new theme unfolds further, the first violin and the cello repeat a two-measure figure five times in the key of E♭ minor, while the basses ascend chromatically until a new transition passage is reached. This transition leads to a final section in which the winds repeat the first tutti in E♭ major. The full orchestra brings this section to a close in E♭ major with the basses playing the frequently mentioned echo of the principal motive.

The principal motive appears again in its initial form to begin the second part of the movement, but it has been transposed up a third and is presented by the clarinets and horns. Passages from the first part of the movement reappear in F minor, C minor, and G minor, but are positioned and orchestrated differently. Finally, after a transition which once again is composed of two-measure phrases, this time with the violins and wind instruments alternating within each two-measure unit—a transition in which the cellos execute a figure in contrary motion to the upper parts while the basses climb upwards—the following chords for full orchestra appear: [mm. 168–79]. They are sounds which purge the breast of a presentiment of the colossal—a presentiment which had wrung it and alarmed it. Like a friendly form that moves through the clouds shining and illuminating the deep night, a theme now enters which had only been suggested by the horn passage in E♭ major at m. 59[5] in the first part of the movement. First in G major, then in C major, the violins carry this theme onward in octaves while the basses execute a descending figure which reminds one to a certain extent of the tutti passage that appeared in m. 44 of the first part of the movement [mm. 179–86]. The wind instruments take up this theme fortissimo in F minor, but after the third measure the strings appropriate the last two measures. Then the winds and strings in turn imitate these last two measures five times, before they alternately play single chords and effect a diminuendo. After the $\frac{6}{3}$ chord, [on f] the reviewer would have expected a G♭-minor chord to appear in the harmonic progression. In the present context, i.e. modulation to G major, the G♭-minor chord could be considered enharmonically as F♯ minor. However, the wind instruments that play the chord following that $\frac{6}{3}$ chord are written:

Immediately thereafter the strings play the F♯-minor chord [f♯–a–c♯¹], which is repeated four times, the winds alternating with the strings in one-measure units. The chords for the winds continue to be written as cited above—a practice for which the reviewer can find no reason. Now, becoming softer and softer, the $\frac{6}{3}$ chord [on f♯], follows directly. This again has a frightening and foreboding effect. The full orchestra then breaks in with a unison G-major theme that is almost exactly the same as the one which entered forty-one measures earlier except that this time the flute and the trumpet hold out the dominant D. By the fourth measure, however, this theme is put aside and the strings, together with the horns, alternate pianissimo with the other winds in playing the diminished seventh chord [on B], seven times. The basses seize upon the initial principal motive in the next measure, the other instruments playing in unison. For five measures the bass and upper voices are in imitation, for the next three they join forces, and in the following the full orchestra with trumpets and timpani announces the prin-

5. Hoffman's text reads "measure 58," an obvious error. [*Editor*]

cipal theme in its original form. The first part of the movement is now repeated with only slight changes. The theme that formerly began in E♭ major now enters in C major and leads to a jubilant C major close with trumpets and timpani. However, within the closing passage itself, the movement turns toward F minor. For five measures the $\frac{6}{3}$ chord [on f], is sounded by the full orchestra. Clarinets, bassoons, and horns play an inversion, piano, of the principal motive. There is one measure of general pause followed by six measures of [a diminished seventh chord on f♯]. This time the imitation of the principal motive is played by all wind instruments. Then the violas, cellos, and bassoons take up a theme that appeared earlier in G major in the second part of the movement, while the violins, entering in unison in the third measure, play a new countermelody. The movement now remains in C minor. With slight changes, the theme, which began in m. 71 in the first part of the movement, is repeated first by the violins alone and then by the violins in alternation with the winds. The alternation becomes closer and closer—first one measure, then a half measure. One senses tremendous force and pressure—a swelling stream whose waves strike higher and higher—which reaches a climax in the repetition of the opening of the Allegro twenty-four measures before the end of the movement. The principal theme is imitated over a pedal point, and the rest of the concluding section follows with strength and power.

There is no simpler motive than that on which the master based the entire Allegro [mm. 1–2]. With great admiration, one becomes aware that Beethoven knew how to relate all secondary ideas and all transition passages through the rhythm of that simple motive so as gradually to unfold the character of the whole work—a character which the principal motive could only suggest. All phrases are short, consisting of only two or three measures, and are distributed to the strings and winds in constant alternation. One would think that something only fragmentary and difficult to grasp could arise from such elements. Instead, it is precisely the ordering of the whole and the constant succession of the repetitions of short phrases and individual chords that holds the heart firmly in unspeakable longing. Completely apart from the fact that the contrapuntal treatment evidences deep study of the art, one can see from the transition passages and the constant allusion to the principal theme that the whole work with all its salient features did not simply flow freely from the master's mind, but was carefully thought through.

As the beautiful voice of a spirit which fills our breast with comfort and hope, the lovely (yet substantial) theme of the Andante[6] in A♭ major and 3/8 meter is now intoned by the viola and the cello. As the Andante unfolds, we are reminded of many middle movements in the symphonies of Haydn. Here, as so frequently in the Haydn movements, several variations of the principal theme are separated by transition passages. Its originality is not on the same level as that of the first Allegro although the idea of having a stately passage with trumpets and timpani enter in C major in a movement constantly moving into and out of A♭ major has a striking effect. Twice the transition to C is effected by the enharmonic modulation:

whereupon the stately theme enters. The modulation back to A♭ major which leads to the dominant chord takes place as follows:

More simply, but with great effect, the flutes, oboes, and clarinets prepare the third transition to the C–major theme:

All the themes of the Andante are very melodious. The principal theme is even soothing. However, the very direction of this theme, which passes through A♭ major, B♭ minor, F minor, and again B♭ minor before returning to A♭; the constant juxtaposition of the keys of A♭ major and C major; and the chromatic modulations reveal once again the

6. Beethoven specifies "Andante con moto." [*Editor*]

character of the whole work and establish the Andante as a part of that whole. It is as if the frightful spirit which seized and tormented our hearts during the Allegro, threatening every moment from the thunder-clouds into which it disappeared, were to step forward, and the friendly spirits which, surrounding us, gave comfort were to flee in haste from its sight.

The Menuett[7] which follows the Andante again demonstrates the originality and the ability to move the listener that one would expect from the master in composing this section of the sym-phony—the section which, in the Haydnesque form adhered to, should be the most clever and piquant of the symphony. It is chiefly the peculiar modulations, the cadences on the major dominant chord whose fundamental tone the bass appropriates for the tonic of the following minor theme, and the theme itself—a theme which is always being extended by just a few measures—that reveal the character of Beetho-ven's music as the reviewer has described it above, and arouse anew that alarm, those premonitions of the realm of the spirits, with which the passages of the Allegro assailed the listener's heart. The C-minor theme carried forward solely by the basses turns toward G minor in the third measure. The horns sustain G, and the violins and violas, in the second measure with the bassoons and later with the clarinets, play a four-measure phrase which cadences in G. The basses now repeat the theme, but after the third measure, G minor leads to D minor and then to C minor, and the violins' phrase is repeated. The horns now play a phrase which moves into E♭ major while the strings play chords in quarter notes at the beginning of every measure. The orchestra leads the movement on into E♭ minor and lands in the dominant, B♭ major. In the same measure the bass begins the principal theme in B♭ minor and performs it as at the beginning when it was in C minor. The violins, etc., also repeat their phrase, and we come to rest in F major. The bass repeats the principal theme but extends it while running through F minor, C minor, and G minor before returning to C minor. Then the tutti that first occurred in E♭ major leads the movement through F minor to the C-major chord. As in the former transition from B♭ major to B♭ minor, the bass now seizes the fundamental tone C as tonic of the theme in C minor. Flutes and oboes, with the imitation of the clarinet in the second measure, now have the phrase which was first played by string instruments, while the latter repeatedly play a measure of the tutti just

7. Beethoven indicates only Allegro. [*Editor*]

mentioned. The horns sustain G while the cellos begin a new theme, which first accompanies a further development of the beginning phrase of the violins and later is companion to an eighth-note passage (which had not appeared before this time). The new theme, itself, contains suggestions of the principal theme. These suggestions, together with rhythmic similarity, relate the new theme in an intimate fashion to the principal theme. After a short repetition of the tutti, the Menuett closes in C minor, fortissimo, with trumpets and timpani sounding. The basses begin the second part (the Trio) with a C-major theme that is imitated in fugal fashion, first in the dominant by the violas, then in shortened form by the second violin, and subsequently, again in shortened form, by the first violin. The first half of the Trio closes in G major. In the second half, the basses begin the theme twice but come to a halt each time. The third time, however, they continue. To many people this may seem playful, but for the reviewer a sinister feeling was awakened. After many imitations of the principal theme, the flutes, supported by the oboes, clarinets, and bassoons, play it over the G pedal note sustained by the horns. The theme dies away in single notes, which are played first by the clarinets with the bassoons and later by the basses. A repetition of the Menuett theme now follows in the basses. This time the winds instead of the violins have the next phrase but with shortened note values; the phrase ends with a pause. At this point as in the original statement of the Menuett, the principal theme is extended, but instead of half notes there are now quarter notes with quarter rests. Most of the other phrases occurring in the original statement of the Menuett also return with notes shortened in this way. The restless yearning which the theme carried with it is now heightened to a fear which tightly constricts the breast permitting only fragmentary, disconnected sounds to escape; the G-major chord seems to lead to the close, but then the basses sustain the A♭ pedal note pianissimo for fifteen measures, and the violins and violas sustain the third, C, while the kettledrum strikes C first in the rhythm of the frequently mentioned tutti, then once per measure for four measures, then twice per measure for four measures, and subsequently in quarter notes. Finally the first violin appropriates the first theme and carries it for twenty-eight measures, until the seventh of the dominant of the fundamental tone is reached. The second violin and the viola have sustained C during this time, the kettledrum has played a C in quarter notes, and the bass has played the G pedal note after having made a chromatic descent from A♭ to F♯ followed by a return to A♭. Not until now do the bassoons, fol-

lowed a measure later by the oboes and then three measures later by the
flutes, horns, and trumpets, enter while the kettledrum strikes C continually in eighth notes. This passage leads directly into the C-major chord
that begins the final Allegro. Why the master allowed the dissonant C of
the kettledrum to continue to the end is explained by the character he
was striving to give to the whole work. The dull, hollow strokes, having
the effect of a strange, frightening voice by their dissonance, arouse the
terror of the extraordinary, of the fear of spirits. Earlier the reviewer
mentioned the mounting effect created by the extensions of the Menuett
theme. To give the reader a clearer view of this effect, these extensions
are displayed together:

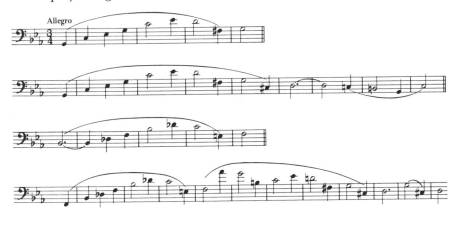

With the return of the Menuett section, this phrase appears in the
following form:

In   the   Menuett,   the   theme   with   which   the   tutti   enters,

is just as simple, and yet, when it emerges again in later passages, is just
as moving as the theme of the first Allegro.

The full orchestra, with piccolos, trombones, and contrabassoon
added, joins in the statement of the magnificent, jubilant, C-major theme

of the final movement. It is like radiant, blinding sunlight which suddenly illuminates the dark night. The phrases of this Allegro are more broadly treated than preceding phrases; they are not so much melodious as they are powerful and suitable for contrapuntal imitation. The modulations are both plain and clear. The first section, especially, almost has the feel of an overture. For thirty-four measures this C-major section remains a tutti for the full orchestra. Then a new theme in the upper voice modulates toward G major by leading toward the dominant chord of this key, while the basses play a powerful, rising figure. Another new theme, consisting of quarter notes interspersed with triplets, now enters. With respect to its rhythm and character, this theme differs completely from the earlier ones and presses forward with the great force exhibited by the theme of the first Allegro and the Menuett [mm. 44-49]. As this theme is stated and makes its way through A minor toward C major, the heart again experiences that foreboding which had been momentarily set aside by the exultation and jubilation. With a short rustling tutti, the movement turns again toward G major, and the violas, bassoons, and clarinets begin a theme in sixths, which the full orchestra takes up farther on. After a short modulation to F minor, leading to a powerful figure in the basses which the violins subsequently play in C major and the basses then take up again *al rovescio*,[8] the first part of the final movement closes in C major. The figure just mentioned reappears in A minor[9] at the beginning of the second part of the movement, and the characteristic theme consisting of quarter notes and triplets also returns. In abbreviated and restricted forms, the theme is now developed for thirty-four measures.[10] In this development, the character of the theme—a character which had already begun to emerge from the theme in its original form—is completely worked out. To this end, no small contribution is made by the attendant secondary phrases, the sustained tones of the trombones, and the second beat triplets of the timpani, trumpets, and horns. The passage finally comes to rest on a G pedal point which is played first by the basses and later, when the basses and violins play a closing figure in unison, by the bass trombone, trumpets, horns, and timpani. Now the simple theme from the Menuett reappears for fifty-

8. I.e. in the opposite direction (downwards); see m. 84. [*Editor*]

9. More literally: on the dominant of what is first A major; see mm. 86ff. [*Editor*]

10. Did not Hoffmann mean thirty-two measures? Mm. 90–121 provide one kind of development; then, with m. 122, a freer rhythmic derivation begins, lasting until m. 132. [*Editor*]

four measures; it is derived from the last two measures of the first transition from the Menuett to the Allegro, but is more restricted. Remaining in the main key but with slight changes, the themes of the first part of the movement return, and a rustling tutti seems to lead to the close. After the dominant chord, however, the bassoons, horns, flutes, oboes, and clarinets, one after another, play a theme which had only been touched on before [mm. 26 ff. and mm. 232 ff.], and the result is another closing passage.[11] This theme is taken up again by the strings, then by the oboes, clarinets, and horns, and finally by the violins. The movement again proceeds toward a close, but with the final chord on the tonic, the violins begin a Presto (a few measures earlier the marking Più stretto[12] had already appeared) with the theme which had presented itself in m. 64 of the Allegro. The basses play the same figure that they had in m. 28 of the first Allegro; as has been mentioned above, it is a figure that reminds one strongly of the principal motive, to which it is intimately related rhythmically. The full orchestra (the basses enter a measure later in canonic imitation of the upper voices) leads toward the close with the first theme of the last Allegro; the close ensues forty-one measures later after many magnificent, jubilant figures. Even the closing chords, themselves, are strangely positioned. To be specific, the chord which the listener believes to be the last is followed by a measure of rest, a repetition of the chord, another measure of rest, another repetition of the chord, another measure of rest, the chord repeated once as a quarter note in each of the next three measures, another measure of rest, another repetition of the chord, another measure of rest, and finally a C played in unison by the full orchestra. The perfect calmness which the heart feels as a result of the several closing figures that are linked together is destroyed by these single struck chords and pauses. These last chords make the listener anxious once again and remind him of the striking of single chords in the Allegro of the symphony. They have the effect of a fire which again and again shoots high its bright, blazing flames after one had believed it extinguished.

Beethoven has retained the usual sequence of movements in the symphony. They seem to be linked together in a fantastic way. For many people, the whole work rushes by like an ingenious rhapsody. The heart

---

11. Corrections: m. 322, clarinets enter; m. 324, oboes; m. 334, strings *and contrabassoon*; m. 336, piccolo, oboe, horns. [*Editor*]

12. Beethoven writes *"Sempre più allegro."* [*Editor*]

of every sensitive listener, however, will certainly be deeply and intimately moved by an enduring feeling—precisely that feeling of foreboding, indescribable longing—which remains until the final chord. Indeed, many moments will pass before he will be able to step out of the wonderful realm of the spirits where pain and bliss, taking tonal form, surrounded him. Besides the internal arrangement of the instrumentation, for example, it is particularly the intimate relationship of the individual themes to one another which produces the unity that firmly maintains a single feeling in the listener's heart. In the music of Haydn and Mozart, this unity prevails everywhere. It becomes clearer to the musician when he discovers a common bass pattern in two different phrases, or when the connecting of two movements makes it obvious. A more profound relationship, however, which cannot be described in such terms, is often communicated from the heart to the heart. It is this relationship which prevails among the themes of both Allegro movements and the Menuett and magnificently proclaims the self-possessed genius of the master. The reviewer believes it possible to summarize his judgment of this work of art in a few words by saying that it was conceived by a genius, it was executed with profound self-possession, and it expresses the romantic nature of music very strongly.

No instrument has difficult passages to perform, but only an extremely secure, practiced orchestra can dare attempt this symphony. Any moment in which the slightest mistake were made would irrecoverably ruin the whole work. The constant exchanges between strings and winds, the single chords to be struck after rests, etc., require the highest precision. The conductor, therefore, should be advised to watch his orchestra and to keep it constantly in hand rather than simply to play the first violin part louder than it ought to be played, as is so often the practice. To this end, the copy of the first violin part on which the entrances of the obbligato instruments are indicated is useful.

The engraving is correct and clear. This symphony has appeared in a version for piano, four hands, at the same publishing house * * *. The reviewer is not usually fond of arrangements. It is not to be denied, however, that playing a masterwork that one has previously heard with full orchestra often stimulates the imagination in a lonely room and leads the heart to the same feelings it had once experienced. The great work is delivered by the piano in the same way a great painting is represented by a sketch which the imagination perceives with the colors of the original. The piano arrangement of the symphony has been made with insight and understanding. Considering the limitations of the instrument, the work has been adapted for piano without destroying the characteristics of the original.

HEINRICH SCHENKER

[*Analysis of the First Movement*] †

Heinrich Schenker (1868-1935) was a remarkable Austrian theorist, whose methods of analysis and musical thinking have had a tremendous influence on the writings of many subsequent theorists. First a composer and pianist, he later turned to the theoretical work for which he is justly famous. His writings include articles both on compositional techniques and on specific works, and he also edited many compositions, including the Beethoven piano sonatas. Schenker's preoccupation was with the total shape of a piece as an extension of the tonic triad of the key in which the piece was set.

Included here is Schenker's analysis of the first movement of the Fifth Symphony. Although this analysis represents a relatively early stage of his progress towards a highly linear conception of music (a conception that develops visibly in the course of the analysis of the complete symphony, which was first published in installments between 1921 and 1924), it offers many valuable insights into the structure of the work, at a rather different level from those represented by the Tovey and Hoffman essays.

The sonata form of the first movement is self-evident, as follows:

First subject:	
Antecedent	mm. 1-21
Consequent and modulation	mm. 22-59
Second subject	mm. 60-125
Development	mm. 126-248
Recapitulation	mm. 249-373
Coda	mm. 374-502

EXPOSITION

The main motive of the first movement is not, as has been erroneously assumed until now, merely the two pitches of mm. 1 and 2 of the score:

Ex. 1

† From *Der Tonwille*, I (1921), 27–37. Reprinted with permission of Universal Edition A. G., Vienna. Translation by the editor and F. John Adams, Jr. Material for footnotes 4, 11, 12, and 16 were provided by Professor Allen Forte.

but rather the combination of four pitches in mm. 1-5;

Ex. 2

Because m. 1 of the score must be understood as a weak measure—the repetition of the exposition (see pp. 180-81) shows that it is
the eighth, and thus a weak measure, of the group beginning at m.
118—the motive is four measures long, mm. 2-5, with m. 1 as an upbeat.
Here is an overall view of the primary transformations of the main motive:

Ex. 3

The first version—Ia, with repeated notes in its upbeat measure and its
second measure [i.e. in the first and third measures of the work] and
with fermatas in its first and fourth measures—is the most powerful version, and serves as the introductory motto for the first subject group; as
the most powerful version, it returns at the beginning of the recapitulation and also toward the end of the coda, in order to establish musical
rhyme, as it were, with the beginning of the movement.

    The second version, Ib, retains the definitive skips of a third found
in the first version, but the fermatas are gone and the repeated notes in

its second measure are replaced by a half note. Being so closely related to
the first version, it is called upon to herald the latter's return, both at the
beginning of the recapitulation and in the coda. The second version
therefore appears toward the end of the development, and then in mm.
399ff., first with the original half notes and immediately thereafter (mm.
407ff.) in diminution.

In IIa we see the second principal form: it differs from Ia by the
substitution of skips of a fifth for those of a third, but (like Ib) it dis-
penses with the fermatas as well as with the repeated notes of the second
measure. It is the lead motto of the second subject-group; consequently it
also opens the second section of the development at mm. 180ff. and pro-
vides the material for thematic elaboration soon afterwards in mm.
195ff.—see version IIb.

It is clear from the initial skip of a third that version Ic is related to
the first principal form; but the first fermata has now become super-
fluous, since the second set of repeated notes has already entered in the
first full measure. Also, a small offshoot [Id] occurs at mm. 23-24; because

Ex. 4

of the initial leap of a third, this relates to the first principal form, and it introduces the consequent of the first idea.

An association of four different pitches is already evident in Beethoven's first sketches for the Fifth Symphony[1].

But Nottebohm's comment about this sketch is incorrect:

> From the standpoint of rhythmic shape, the four-note main motive of the first movement of the Symphony in C Minor is also contained in the main theme of the first movement of the Piano Concerto in G Major. In the concerto it appears as an isolated motive in a primitive version; here, as a part of a larger melodic whole. The sketches show us that the primitive version was the early one and preceded the other setting.

In both cases, in the Symphony and the Piano Concerto—the theme of which is as follows:[2]

Ex. 5

—a distinction must be made between repetition, in the service of only a single tone, and the main motive taken as a whole, consisting of several pitches. The harmonic successions indicated in Ex. 4 demonstrate this very well, since pitch-repetition never enters the question at all, but rather, to use Nottebohm's phrase, "a larger melodic whole"—specifically four pitches and four measures.

The same harmonic argument applies to Beethoven's final version for if one were to hear the motive as complete at the first fermata, then it would follow that the third G–E♭ would have to be understood first of all as the tonic of E♭ major—an idea that certainly would not occur to anyone.

That Beethoven intended the four-measure character of the main motive is also demonstrated by a correction which he subsequently supplied for the first printing. He still writes as follows in the final score:

1. *NBv.*, p. 10 ff.; cf. above, p. 117. [*Editor*]
2. *NBv.*, p. 12. [*Editor*]

This notation preserves the basic metrical plan of four and two, as at Ia and Id, so that the next motive is adjoined in either the fourth or the second measure (as with the upbeat). The two-measure grouping is given unequivocally at Ic. He subsequently appended a measure to each of these passages in order to obtain the grouping of four or two for the motive itself, regardless of whether the next measure is incorporated as an upbeat (as at Ia and Id) or as a fourth measure in the regular way (as at Ic). The upbeat character of the first three eighth notes in m. 1 of the score is extended not only to the regular formations (for example at mm. 14, 22, 29, 101, etc.) but also to some (such as mm. 6, 25, 390) which are, so to speak, filled to excess.

Certainly the most convincing proofs of the cohesiveness of mm. 1-5 in the motivic sense are shown by the Basic Line [*Urlinie*] (pp. 180-81). From this we see that not even all four pitches of the principal motive (see Ex. 3) are significant to the Basic Line, but only the two half notes separated by the step of a second. Grouping by twos and the distance of a second remain as earmarks of the motive, even when, as in IIa, a more distant note is substituted (Bb for D). Mm. 26-29, and then (leaving out the suspension constructions in mm. 34-35ff.) mm. 45-48, 49-51, 60, etc., each reply with two tones a second part.

This proof is confirmed and strengthened by the following illustration:

Ex. 6

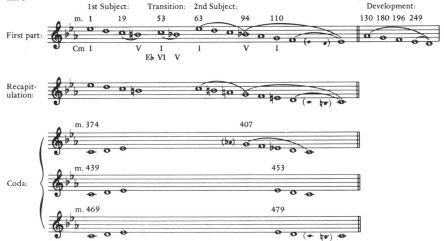

This diagram—certainly the primary formulation of the creative fantasy, of which the Basic Line (below) represents a kind of first elaboration— shows how clearly the two kernel tones of the motive, even after being filled out with additional tones, still strive toward the nodal points of the fourth or fifth.[3] Were the principal motive still to be understood as it had been previously, the Basic Line and the barest preliminary shape would lead one to the extremely remarkable conclusion that a motive could consist of a single note: but if a motive is to have melodic value, must it not consist of a succession of several notes, or at least of two notes? (The rhythmic motive is another matter, of course, which is not affected by the question of pitch difference.) It should be remembered that even in the case of Id (Ex. 3) Beethoven preserves the two-measure grouping for the single note F, and, moreover, places this note immediately at the head of the two-note main motive.[4]

That it was previously possible to misconstrue the main motive, an understanding of which is certainly a prerequisite for performance and enjoyment, is attributable to the repeated notes (it is odd that even those musicians who turn up their noses at four-measure patterns in music do not recognize a four-measure plan even when it is presented to them by Beethoven). By themselves, repeated notes suggest the sympathetically resonating sound of one or more spoken words[5]; if there is added to this, as in the case of our symphony, the fermata and the continuation in the

3. At this point, Schenker refers to his (then) as yet unpublished *Der freie Satz*, the concluding portion of his *Neue musikalische Theorien und Phantasien* (Vienna, 1935). The section to which he refers, on "Quart- und Quint-Knotenpunkte" (nodal points of the fourth and fifth), does not appear in the book as it was finally published. Apparently Schenker abandoned the term "nodal point" (*Knotenpunkt*) after this; it seems to be used in the sense of a "point of linkage" between linear progressions. [*Editor*]

4. It is probably not immediately clear to the reader what Schenker means here. The important term is "two-note motive." His analysis of the theme, as shown on pp. 180–81, shows E♭ and D as the main notes; these comprise the "two-note motive." Thus, his comment on the placement of F at the head of the two-note motive might be elucidated as follows:

m. 25 2-note motive F-E♭ (*cf.* Ex. 6)

2-note motive E♭-D

In the Basic Line, Schenker brackets many occurrences of the two-note motive. [*Editor*]

5. As I have shown in my *Kontrapunkt* (*Neue musikalische Theorien und Phantasien*, II), Vienna, 1910, pp. 63ff.

adjoining measures, the unpracticed ear receives the impression of a motive already completed by the first fermata. Furthermore, it was the repeated notes that inspired the growth of legends. One has only to recall Czerny, for example, who claimed—allegedly on the basis of a remark by Beethoven—that the rhythmic motive was based on the call of the yellow-hammer,[6] or Schindler, who claimed—also allegedly according to an utterance of Beethoven—that the figure referred to the dominating power of Fate over man ("Thus Fate knocks at the door") ,[7] to pass judgment on the utter worthlessness of such statements. The dangerously enticing adherence of a Richard Wagner to the camp of those who consider mm. 1-2 as the motive only proves that he, a complete stranger to absolute music, succumbed to the mysterious eloquence of the repeated notes no less than did Czerny, Schindler, and others. In his essay *On Conducting* he writes[8]:

> Now suppose we could hear Beethoven calling from his grave to the conductor, "Make my fermatas long and formidable. I do not write fermatas in sport or out of hesitation as to what to express next. The tone in my Adagio, which is to be completely and fully experienced in order that expression be given to a luxurious feeling, is used, when I need it, in a rapid and violent Allegro, to create a rapturous or frightening spasm. There the life-blood of the note must be squeezed out to the last drop. There I hold back the waves of my sea and allow a view into its depths; or I restrain the movement of the clouds, split apart the swirling mists, and allow a glimpse of the pure blue sky and of the radiant eye of the sun! This is why I place fermatas, i.e. the sudden notes which are to be sustained for a long time, in my Allegros. Now consider what completely definite thematic purpose I had with this sustained E♭ after three tempestuous short notes, and what I wanted to say with all the following notes that are likewise to be sustained."

Even supposing that in the master's imagination there had been an association of ideas between the rhythm of the motive and Fate knocking on the door, it is the obligations of art, not of Fate, that are discharged in the motive's development. And if one wanted to deduce on hermeneutic grounds that Beethoven is struggling with Fate the whole movement long, into the struggle would go not Fate alone, but also Beethoven; not

6. See F. Kerst, ed., *Die Erinnerungen an Beethoven*, 2 vols., Stuttgart, 1913. I, 54. On the other hand, Schindler tells the same story in connection with the second movement of the Sixth Symphony; see Schindler, *Beethoven as I Knew Him*, ed. Donald W. McArdle, transl. Constance S. Jolly, Chapel Hill, 1966, pp. 144-45. [*Editor*]

7. See below, p. 185. [*Editor*]

8. For this passage in a fuller context (and a different translation), see below, pp. 192-93. [*Editor*]

just Beethoven the man, but, even more, Beethoven the musician. Even if Beethoven were struggling thus in notes, no hermeneutical explanation and none of the legends are sufficient to explain the world of notes unless one thinks and feels with these notes, so to speak, according to their own laws. Anyone who, in spite of all this, would for the sake of the legends still balk at discarding musical and metrical nonsense, need only consider that Beethoven used a similar note-repetition, after all, in the [Fourth] Piano Concerto. Was that, perhaps, a different door on which Fate was knocking, or the same door but a different kind of knocking?

One cannot deny, in any case, that the reasonable ease with which the motive of our symphony can be grasped—Grove calls it a "sympathetic" motive,[9] and motive-counters may verify how often it recurs— wins the listener's affection from its very first appearance. The great number of repetitions was undoubtedly the main source of enjoyment, it seems, for those who take pleasure directly from hearing and experiencing how many times they can recognize a motive's recurrence. If even this surely very minor achievement could create so much satisfaction, one might logically assume that a greater mental accomplishment would lead to even greater satisfaction. How happy the listener would be if he could share with the master his long-range hearing, and travel and soar with him over distant paths! If he only could! Then his fear that better hearing might encroach somewhat on his pleasure would give way to rapture.

It only remains to be said that, as regards the closed four-measure construction of the main motive, the fermatas are merely an internal concern; that in the strictest sense they could after all be eliminated both at the beginning and in other passages—just as they are, for example, at the statement in mm. 228 ff. To be sure, they increase the energy and strengthen the effect of the repeated notes, which they heighten, as it were, to an imploring shout—but far beyond these effects soars the cohesive power that creates bonds on an even higher level by using four— indeed, basically only two—principal notes.

The motivic formation that first appears at m. 14 in the first violins represents a passing motion through the same interval of a third that the main motive (mm. 1-2) had already spanned; yet it also forms a thematic element in its own right, as is particularly confirmed in the development.

9. Schenker writes "sympathischer," but does not give a source. In his *Beethoven and his Nine Symphonies*, London, 1896, Grove refers to the opening theme as possessing "prodigious originality, form, and conciseness" (p. 138), and as "most famous" (p. 141). On p. 145 he states: "It would be sublime if there were not too much conflict in it, and if it contained the religious element." [*Editor*]

It is precisely the downward thrust of this passing motion that forces the notes still farther in the same direction to the nodal point of a fourth (see Ex. 6 above).

One may observe the variation in the rhythmic position of the main motive's second half note: at first, as in mm. 4 and 11, it falls respectively on the third measure of a four-measure group and on the fifth measure of an eight-measure group—i.e. on relatively strong measures. However, this natural pattern is breached in the eight-measure group, mm. 26-33, where the second half note [in this case represented by an eighth note, the E♭s in mm. 29 and 33] is stated on the fourth and eighth measures—i.e. the weakest ones. Matters reach the point that the basic metrical pattern in the next ten-measure group, mm. 34-43, which merely mediates between the following chords:

Ex. 7

mm. 34 — 44

becomes loosened, so much do the two halves of the motive deviate even further from their rhythmic equilibrium. One observes their position in the second, fifth, sixth, and eighth measures of the group in mm. 44-51, and in the second and seventh measures of the group in mm. 52-59, which throughout give the impression of a reiteration of the notes of the motive against the bass. Scarcely noticeable at first, all these disruptions of equilibrium gradually become more and more dizzying in the excitement of modulation, but, in conformity with a general law of nature, they finally press back again towards order and restraint.

Variety, too, is operative, since the compositional thought in the antecedent (from m. 7 on) is carried by upward arpeggiation, but in the consequent by downward arpeggiation.

In contrast to the first subject, the second, from the formal standpoint, runs its course unbroken. It traverses the octave from e♭² to e♭¹ (as can be seen in Ex. 6), divided naturally into a descent of a fourth and a descent of a fifth. The first of these is an imitation of the fourth-descent in mm. 17-21, and the fifth-descent is its necessary inversionary extension. In the working-out, to be sure, the nodal point of b♭¹ is placed an octave higher (m. 94), and therefore the fifth-descent is completed by the double-stopped octave. The beginning and end of the fourth-descent (mm. 63-66) stand within the tonic chord [i.e. of the relative major]; but after the high b♭² has been reached in m. 94, the dominant takes command in the next two eight-measure groups (see their respective beginnings and ends in mm. 94 and 101, 102 and 109). Since within this section the g^2 (in mm. 96 and 104) still occurs on the third—thus, weak—measure of the group, the tonic at this point is too weak to impede the predominance of the dominant. Thus g^2 is purposefully brought in once again in m. 110, at the outset of the next eight-measure group, which carries out the last part of the fifth-descent in a broader dimension, so to speak; now the tonic takes the lead for the final decisive emphasis. What an ingenious conception for the ground plan of the second subject!

It has already been pointed out (Ex. 3) that in the lead motto of the second subject the note b♭ really stands for d^1. This substitution accomplishes two things: the concealed second, $e♭^1$–d^1, pushes outward, as in mm. 15ff., to the nodal point of the fourth, while the substituted b♭ itself proclaims and confirms this in advance. Only such an interpretation prevents the motive of the first violins in mm. 63-65 from being heard as an exact variant of the introductory motto, as it might seem to be upon superficial consideration because of the extension up to f^2 (m. 65) and the descent to $b♭^1$ (m. 66) ; one sees instead that it is rather a variant of the fourth-descent, as the Basic Line (below) makes clear. In what follows, too, the fourth-descent is repeated several times and the variation becomes perfectly clear in this direction. The shape of the Basic Line also makes evident how, at the same time that there is motion from I to IV (mm. 74-82), the fourth e♭–a♭ is traversed by means of passing tones in the bass; how, then, within the ♮IV (mm. 84-93), a passing motion in the bass pushes to the third of the harmony (m. 90) ; and, finally, how, by an exchange, the a of the bass (m. 84) ascends to the $b♭^2$ of the soprano (m. 94), while conversely the diminished fifth of the harmony, $e♭^2$ (m. 85), descends to d in the bass.

The introductory motto of the second subject, with its emphatic expression, reestablishes contact with the metrical scheme that had been broken during the modulation: the half notes E♭ and B♭ appear again in the first and third measures of the group. But since the first note (E♭) of the fourth-motive begins already in the fourth measure, a new friction with the meter begins immediately, one that in its turn must be overcome. All this is also mirrored in the phrasing—what genius is shown in the creation of such relationships!—which strengthens and underscores both friction and resolution.

Thus, if the variant of the fourth-motive, in contrast to the horn call, is to be played legato, then obviously its upbeat measure (m. 63) should be included under the slur, and, further, the slur must break between mm. 65 and 66 because of the adjacent c²s. The change in the variant that occurs from m. 75 on because of the altered harmonic relationships, and during which the juxtaposition of two identical tones also disappears, requires another bowing: namely, the connection of a weak measure to a strong one (see the shorter slurs in the Basic Line, mm. 75-82) so frequently used by Beethoven for expressive purposes.[10]

With the expansion of the ♮IV (mm. 84-93) the delay of the last note of the linear progression through the fourth, namely d—which delay is indeed the purpose of the expansion—requires still another new and characteristic style of bowing.

Ex. 8

Indeed, as the expansion begins, mm. 83-85 are grouped together in the manner of mm. 63-65. However, since the expansion can hardly be misunderstood [i.e., as anything other than an expansion] as long as the final tone (d) is absent, it was even ventured (in order to prepare for the equalization of meter which occurs at the onset of the linear progression of a fifth in a good register, with b♭² in m. 94) to bring in the head of the motive, g♭², on relatively strong measures of the group (mm. 86, 88, 90, and 92) and even to begin the slur on g♭² and thus bring it into accord with the motivic kernel. From this, one realizes that, in order to achieve precisely this type of phrasing, it was necessary to group the first three measures (mm. 83-85) so as to distinguish them from the previous style of phrasing (mm. 75-82).[11] But to repeat something like this four times in succession—at mm. 86, 88, 90, and 92—obviously seemed disturbing to the master, and he felt obliged, first, to place a slur over two

10. See Schenker, *Monographie über die IX Sinfonie von Beethoven*, Vienna, 1912, pp. 40–42, and his *Die letzten fünf Sonaten von Beethoven: Erläuterungsausgaben*, Vienna, 1914, IV (Op. 110), 37, etc.

11. What Schenker is saying is only this: in the previous eight measures (mm. 75–82) the phrasing is in twos, viz. ♩ ♩|♩ ♩|♩ ♩|♩ ♩|♩ ♩ ♩

Thus, to show that a new event (the expansion) is beginning, the phrasing is changed in mm. 83–85 to ♩ ♩|♩ ♩|♩ ♩ ♩ . [*Editor*]

measures (86-87) and then—beginning right in the middle of the group and thereby, so to speak, preserving its balance—to have the remaining six measures (88-93) all under one slur. On the other hand, however, in order not to endanger the crescendo effect by too long a slur, he breaks the slur in the cellos (who play the same line) into two, spanning two and four measures respectively, and at m. 91 he adds the flute, which joins in for the last three measures under one slur. The irregular ten-measure arrangement of the extension, as well as the unusual manner of phrasing, lends to this passage an ineffable, irresistible magic.

The reasons why the groups of the second subject have been articulated as shown in the Basic Line, and not otherwise, are as follows: it is clear that the horn call, because it spans the interval of a fourth and confirms the meter (see above), is disassociated from the material that follows. Of the three statements of the by now very familiar fourth-motive that follow, the first two can conveniently be separated as simply an extended reinforcement, and treated as an eight-measure group, almost as if they had no great importance in what follows. Thus it is not until the third repetition (mm. 71-74) that the real point of departure for the upward movement is presented. If we were to balance the twelve measures 72-83 (three groups of four measures) against the subsequent ten (84-93), we would misconstrue the meaning and affect of the extension, which can only be realized when we view it rather as an initial eight-measure group (72-79) superseded by a group of fourteen measures (80-93).

Ex. 6 shows the ultimate background of the development, summed up as a diminished chord on II (or VII) in C minor. In the Basic Line the path is manifest in the clear grouping of three distinct sections, beginning at mm. 130, 180, and 196, with the notes A♭, G, and F respectively as, so to speak, stopping places within the span of the diminished fifth.

Before the first part, the introductory motto of the first subject is established while a chromatic modulation from E♭ to F minor is effected:

Ex. 9

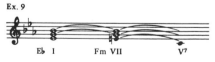

thereby defining the material in terms of what preceded. In fact, the two-note main motive is taken up in this section in the same way as in the first subject (mm. 137-38 = mm. 14-15). In mm. 142-45 the descending quarter notes[12] exceed the original span of a fourth (cf. mm. 17-21); yet in this elongation they seem to stem rather from the octave-descent in mm. 94-101, just as the ascending counterpoint in the lower voice probably derives in a similar fashion from the ascending bass line in those same measures.

The passage modulates from F minor to C minor. In C minor an inversion of the two voices takes place; the passage modulates further, to G minor. A recovery of the original voice-placement in G minor is then completed in the next measure-group (154ff.), by means of an expansion from the half-cadence in G minor. The soprano line that rises beginning in m. 158 should be interpreted as an enlargement of the line in mm. 150-53; as the Basic Line shows, the soprano is also furnished with anticipations. At m. 167 the falling line (cello and viola) accelerates in eighths, with the result that m. 168, whose content is different from the expected anticipation, now becomes a strong measure of a new group, as a result of this very change. Here there is a change of tonal center: IV with assimilated passing tones goes through ♮IV (mm. 172-75) to V in m. 176.

The soprano line, which rises beginning in m. 158, can be reduced basically to a succession of only three notes:

M.	158		162		166
	B♭	–	C	–	D
	I		–		V

if one disregards the almost turn-like detour (E♭–E–D–C♯) before the final d[3] (mm. 168-79). If one realizes, however, that the descent of the line can be traced back in abbreviated form to m. 130 as in the following:

Ex. 10

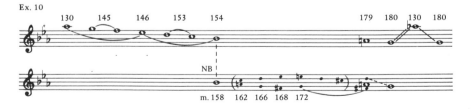

12. Schenker's reference to quarter notes here becomes clear when compared with the Basic Line (pp. 180–81); he is referring to his reduction of the passage, rather than to its foreground manifestation in eighth notes. [*Editor*]

then one sees that in a still deeper sense d³ here at m. 179 substitutes for a², another note of the dominant chord, and that the ascent to d³ has been undertaken precisely in order to prepare for the leap of a fifth required for the beginning of the introductory motto that follows. Ex. 10 shows, moreover, not only the first fourth-descents, which are still in operation, but also the path from the primary note (A♭) of the first part to the primary note (G) of the second; see Ex. 6.

The second part of the development starts at m. 180 with the introductory motto of the second subject group. The second note of the main motive, which in both the first and second versions (Ia and IIa in Ex. 3) has merely the significance of a neighbor note as far as the basic line is concerned, is led back in this section to the passing motion that is concealed in every neighbor note.[13] Thus a² (m. 181) rises finally to b² (m. 187) just as in the next eight-measure group d² (m. 189) rises to e² (m. 195). So there develop nodal points a fourth apart, out of which— here led by the strings—a continually rising line develops.

Ex. 11

Consequently we arrive, in m. 196, at the note f². In this passage, the F chord can already be heard as IV of the principal tonality, and its dominant needs to be reached. In a powerful transitional construction, full of the marvel of synthesis, the line (ascending as in both previous eight-measure groups, but led this time by the winds) traverses the path f² to e♭²:

Ex. 12

The diagrams on p. 178 may serve to clarify the transitional construction. Ex. 13a shows the simplest way to avoid a parallel fifth: the rise from IV♯³ to V♯³ is accomplished through the change 5-6 and the use of chromatics. If the initial triad has a minor third, as in Ex. 13b, the reduction to this minor third makes possible an expansion of the path,[14]

13. See Schenker, *Kontrapunkt*, p. 240.
14. To the F♯-A-D chord. [*Editor*]

which then resumes the original direction.[15] In Ex. 13c one can see
how the line, by means of anticipations (in which the second note of the
main motive is concealed) is prepared for its upward course. To begin
with, Beethoven pushes towards B♭, the nodal point of a fourth (m.
209), and this only because he also wanted to offer an association with
earlier fourth-progressions—what a categorical imperative of the
ear!—even in the middle of the passing motion. This nodal point of a
fourth thus explains the path over G♭ and A, with the effect of B♭
minor:

$$\frac{\text{mm. 204-209}}{= V \sharp^3\text{-}I\,\flat^3}$$

Ex. 13d shows that the further it ascends, the more hesitant becomes the
course: from note to note the distance increases. By reinterpreting m. 209
as a strong measure (although it was originally weak) followed by a

15. In this connection, a passage in Beethoven's D minor Piano Sonata, Op. 31, No.
2, first movement, mm. 157 ff., also proceeds in this way:

weak m. 210, the nodal point becomes especially underlined, so that from here on there is no longer any difficulty in recognizing that only the winds have the strong measures. Into this state of hesitation and suspended breath, there falls suddenly, with a tremendous force that takes the listener almost completely by surprise, the introductory motto of the first subject group, in the Ib version—in the inner voices. At first, the top line still remains untouched by this outcry. Although the inner voices make their presence known in the heart of the texture, the upper voice does not obey this mortal force until the subsequent groups of measures. More frequent and heavier strokes (see mm. 241-48) are required before the d³ of the upper line completely fades away, and is resurrected anew in the e♭³ (at m. 249) of the initial introductory motto.

The rule of variation in the recapitulation applies to the Fifth Symphony as to all other masterworks; we find not merely a dull restatement, but rather one that breathes with new life because of various details. Thus, as early as the first subject, the bassoon and oboe appear—the latter, in fact, with a solo in m. 268, an embellishment of the fermata, which in terms of a higher technique of symmetry represents the call at mm. 22-24 in the exposition.

In the recapitulation, the opening of the second subject is entrusted to the bassoons rather than the horns. This occurs, as has been said, for the sake of freshness and variety. In contrast to mm. 29-33, the strings in mm. 273-76 sound together in unison. Because of the different harmonic situation, a change in the accompaniment is necessary in mm. 331-45, as compared with mm. 83-93:

Ex. 14

There, an expansion of ♮IVb⁷ occurred, leading only later to V; here it proceeds from the outset on V, where it can take place only with the mixture of the major and minor intervals, A♭ and A.[16] (Although theoretically possible, a parallel mixture of G♭ and G in mm. 83-93 was ruled

16. With respect to the mixture of A♭ and A here. Schenker assumes that the reader will understand that the A♭ is required in order to provide the necessary melodic replication (with respect to the exposition), while the A is required for harmonic reasons. This is why the mixture is unavoidable. [*Editor*]

Fig. 6.

out because the G had to be reserved for the subsequent fifth-progression.) As Ex. 15 shows, the transition from the minor $a\flat^2$ to the major a^2 is made at approximately the middle of the fourteen-measure group. The mixture functions so strongly in itself that no further niceties of phrasing are needed to strengthen this effect.

The coda unfolds in three sections, which are all characterized (cf. the Basic Line and Ex. 6) by a line that each time rises from, and again sinks back to, the tonic note C (see mm. 374, 439, and 469). The arch of the falling line is the most drawn out in the first of these three sections, where it covers the whole span of a fifth, g^2–c^2, in mm. 407-39. This fifth-descent with the minor third answers the fifth-descent in the major in the recapitulation (mm. 346-73). At m. 399 the interpretation of mm. 1-5 as $V^{6\text{-}5}$ is confirmed. The Basic Line especially clarifies the great amount of passing motion in mm. 407-22. The final section has as its purpose the resolution of the ascending leading-tone, just as it had been resolved at the end of the exposition, in a similar way (see Ex. 6).

VIEWS AND COMMENTS

ANTON SCHINDLER[†]

~~~~~~

Anton Schindler (1795-1864) is another example of a man who, like
Hoffmann, wavered between jurisprudence and music. His contact with
Beethoven, beginning in 1814, decided the matter. In 1822 he left the law
to become first violinist at Vienna's Josephstadttheater; but his principal
activity for the last seven years of Beethoven's life was to be his secretary
and general factotum. The first edition of his biography of Beethoven appeared in 1840. The third edition (1860), from which this excerpt is
drawn, was almost completely rewritten.

Thayer discussed Schindler's qualifications as a biographer at length
with Otto Jahn, both men having known him personally: "We held him
to be honest and sincere in his statements, but afflicted with a treacherous
memory and a proneness to accept impressions and later formed convic-
tions as facts of former personal knowledge, and to publish them as such
without carefully verifying them."

In the crown of the master's symphonic creations, the C minor symphony stands next to the *Pastoral*. Indeed, as free poetry which, though
independent of all outer influences, still owes its existence to external
forces, it surpasses the *Pastoral* and represents the greatest triumph in
instrumental music up to that time. Among the hundreds of compositions written by many masters, no work bears out more fully than Beethoven's C minor symphony the maxim that every true work of art is a
realization of the divine, whose purpose it is to confer the loftiest bless-
ing on man by the enlightenment of the earthy and the spiritualization
of the sensual as well as by the sensualization of the spirit. What a mar-
vellous union of pathos, majesty, mystery, and grandeur is contained in
those four movements! What a life of poetry this work unfolds before our
senses, allowing us to see into its depths! The composer himself provided
the key to those depths when one day, in this author's presence, he
pointed to the beginning of the first movement and expressed in these
words the fundamental idea of his work: "Thus Fate knocks at the door!"

† From Anton Schindler, *Beethoven as I Knew Him*, ed. Donald W. McArdle,
transl. Constance S. Jolly, Chapel Hill, 1966, p. 147. Reprinted by permission of The
University of North Carolina Press. First published in Schindler, *Biographie von Ludwig van Beethoven*, 3rd ed., Münster, 1860.

LUDWIG SPOHR[†]

Ludwig Spohr (1784-1859) was a German composer, conductor, and violinist who in the 19th century enjoyed considerable fame and success. In 1812 he came to Vienna for a three-year stay, where his performances in particular attracted great attention. He met Beethoven and recorded some impressions of him in a journal, later incorporated in an autobiography. While he was enthusiastic about Beethoven's early works—he took part in performances of the Op. 18 Quartets—Spohr was cooler about Beethoven's later works, as the following account shows. This journal was kept during one of Spohr's many tours, this time to South and West Germany, Alsace, Switzerland and Italy, right after his stay in Vienna.

Munich, December 12, 1815

Our stay here has been rich in artistic pleasures. On the very day of our arrival we heard an interesting concert, the first of twelve Winter Concerts given each year by the Royal Orchestra for its own benefit. These concerts are well attended, and most deservedly so. The orchestra has twelve first and twelve second violins, eight violas, ten cellos, and six double basses. Violins and basses are excellent, as are also the wind instruments, with the possible exception of the horns. Each concert includes an entire symphony (a practice the more to be praised, as it is growing less and less common and the public is losing its feeling for this noblest of all instrumental forms), then an overture, and two vocal and two instrumental solos. Since the Munich Orchestra still enjoys a reputation as one of the best in the world, my expectations were high, and I hasten to record that in the performance of Beethoven's Symphony in C minor, which opened the concert, they were unsurpassed. It is hardly possible that this symphony could be played with more fire and more strength and, at the same time, with more tenderness and with more precise attention to every nuance. It had, accordingly, a greater effect than I would have thought possible, although I had heard it frequently in Vienna and under the composer's direction. Even so, I found no reason to reverse my earlier judgment. It has many individual beauties, but they do not add up to a classical whole. The very first theme, in particular,

† From *The Musical Journeys of Louis Spohr*, transl. and ed. Henry Pleasants, University of Oklahoma Press, 1961, pp. 125–27. First published in Spohr, *Selbstbiographie*, Cassel and Göttingen, 1860–61, I, 228.

lacks the dignity essential to the opening of a symphony. This aside, however, the short, easily grasped theme lends itself well to thematic elaboration, and the composer has combined it most imaginatively and
effectively with other principal motives of the first movement. The
adagio, in A♭, is very beautiful in part, but the same progressions and
modulations are repeated too often, despite the ever richer figuration.
The scherzo is highly original, and of genuinely romantic texture, but
the trio, with its tumbling bass runs, is too baroque for my taste. The last
movement, with its empty noise, is the least satisfactory, although the
return of the scherzo is such a happy idea that one can only envy the
composer who could have thought of such a thing. It is quite irresistible.
What a pity that the effect is so soon dissipated by the resumption of the
noise.

HECTOR BERLIOZ [†]

Hector Berlioz (1803-69) planned his Memoirs as a correction to what he
considered inaccuracies in the writings of others about himself. The preface was written in 1848, the compilation of notes was continued until
1854, and a postscript was written in 1858, but the book was not published
until 1870. The following account, like the one by Mendelssohn that follows, is touching in its description of the effect that Beethoven's music had
on one who was trying hard to resist it. This account also catches, of
course, the tempestuous feelings that Berlioz had for the majority of his
musical contemporaries.

In an artist's life one thunderclap sometimes follows swiftly on another,
as in those outsize storms in which the clouds, charged to bursting with
electric energy, seem to be hurling the lightning back and forth and
blowing the whirlwind.

I had just had the successive revelations of Shakespeare and Weber.
Now at another point on the horizon I saw the giant form of Beethoven
rear up. The shock was almost as great as that of Shakespeare had been.
Beethoven opened before me a new world of music, as Shakespeare had
revealed a new universe of poetry.

† From *The Memoirs of Hector Berlioz*, transl. and ed. David Cairns, New York,
1969, pp. 104–06. Copyright David Cairns.

The Conservatoire Concert Society had recently been founded[1] under the fervent and vigorous direction of Habeneck.[2] With all his serious defects as a musician and his shortcomings even in the service of his idol, he was a sincere and able conductor; and nothing can take away the glory of having been the man who made Beethoven's works popular in Paris. It is thanks to his efforts that the Conservatoire Society, today famous throughout the civilized world, was founded at all. It was a severe struggle; and before he could secure adequate performances, he had to persuade a large body of players to share his enthusiasm for totally unfamiliar music which had the reputation of being eccentric and difficult to play; he had to overcome an indifference which turned to hostility at the prospect of endless rehearsals and unremunerative toil stretching ahead.

Not the least of Habeneck's troubles was the steady undercurrent of opposition from French and Italian composers, who regarded the whole idea with malicious and ill-concealed disapproval. They had no desire to see official homage paid to a German whose works seemed to them misbegotten monstrosities and yet at the same time a threat to their own style of composition. I have heard them airing the most lamentable nonsense about those marvels of beauty and technical mastery.

In this connection my teacher, Lesueur,[3] an honest man without envy in his nature and devoted to his art, but the prisoner of musical dogmas which I must be allowed to describe as sheer delusion, let slip a significant remark. Although he lived a somewhat retired life, buried in his own work, it was not long before he became aware of the stir which the inauguration of the Conservatoire concerts and the performances of Beethoven's symphonies were causing in the Paris musical world. His surprise was all the greater because like most of his fellow-academicians he considered instrumental music an inferior branch of the art, respectable certainly but of limited importance, in which Haydn and Mozart had in any case gone as far as it was possible to go.

Like the rest of them—like Berton,[4] who regarded the whole of

---

1. 15th February 1828, by decree of the Director of Fine Arts. The first concert (9th March) opened with the Eroica, which was repeated on 23rd March. The Fifth Symphony followed on 13th April. [*Cairns*]

2. François-Antoine Habeneck (1781–1849), French violinist, conductor and composer. [*Editor*]

3. Jean-François Lesueur (1760–1837), French composer, director of the Chapel Royal in Paris, and professor of composition at the Paris Conservatoire from 1818 until his death. [*Editor*]

4. Henri-Montan Berton (1767–1844), French composer, theorist, and teacher, well-known at the time for his opéras-comiques. [*Editor*]

modern German music with pitying contempt; like Boïeldieu,[5] who did not know what to think of it all and expressed a childlike astonishment at any harmonic progression beyond the three chords he had been using all his life; like Cherubini,[6] who choked back his bile and did not openly vent it on a composer whose success exasperated him and undermined his own most cherished theories; Paër,[7] the crafty Italian, who claimed to have known Beethoven, and told stories about him more or less discreditable to the great man and favourable to himself; Catel,[8] who had disagreed with music, and lived only for his garden and his collection of rose-trees; Kreutzer,[9] who shared Berton's contempt for everything that originated beyond the Rhine—Lesueur took no notice. Confronted with the immense enthusiasm of musicians in general and of me in particular, he shut his ears and carefully avoided the Conservatoire concerts. To have gone would have meant committing himself to a personal opinion of Beethoven; it would have meant being physically involved in the tremendous excitement which Beethoven aroused. This was just what Lesueur, without admitting it, did not wish to happen. However, I kept on at him, solemnly pointing out that when something as important as this occurred in our art—a completely new style on an unprecedented scale—it was his duty to find out about it and judge for himself; and in the end he yielded and let himself be dragged off to the Conservatoire one day when the C minor Symphony was being performed. He wanted to give it an unbiased hearing, without distractions of any kind, so he dismissed me and sat by himself at the back of one of the ground-floor boxes, among people he did not know. When it was over I came down from the floor above, eager to know what effect this extraordinary work had had on him and what he thought of it.

I found him in the corridor, striding along with flushed face. "Well, master?"

"Ouf! Let me get out. I must have some air. It's amazing! Wonderful! I was so moved and disturbed that when I emerged from the box and attempted to put on my hat, I couldn't find my head. Now please leave me be. We'll meet tomorrow."

5. François-Adrien Boïeldieu (1775–1834), French operatic composer. [*Editor*]
6. Maria Luigi Cherubini (1760–1842), Italian-born composer, resident in Paris; from 1822 until his death, director of the Paris Conservatoire. [*Editor*]
7. Ferdinando Paër (1771–1839), Italian composer and pianist. [*Editor*]
8. Charles-Simon Catel (1773–1830), French composer and theorist, whose *Traité d'harmonie* was long the standard French textbook on the subject. [*Editor*]
9. Rodolphe Kreutzer (1766–1831), French composer, violinist, and conductor. The composers named in this paragraph comprise a virtual catalogue of Berlioz's *bêtes noires* in the Paris musical world. [*Editor*]

I was triumphant. The next day I hurried round to see him. The conversation at once turned to the masterpiece which had stirred us so profoundly. Lesueur let me talk on for some time, assenting in a rather constrained manner to my exclamations of enthusiasm. But it was easy to see that my companion was no longer the man who had spoken to me the day before, and that he found the subject painful. I persisted, however, until I had dragged from him a further acknowledgement of how deeply Beethoven's symphony had moved him; at which he suddenly shook his head and smiled in a curious way and said, "All the same, music like that ought not to be written."

"Don't worry, master," I retorted, "there is not much danger that it will."

Poor human nature! Poor master! What a world of regret, of stubborn resentment, jealousy, dread of the unknown, confession of incapacity lies behind it and all such remarks made by countless men in similar situations! To say, "Music like that ought not to be written," after having felt its power and being forced to recognize its beauty, is as much as to say that you yourself would never do such a thing—because you know you couldn't even if you wanted to.

FELIX MENDELSSOHN[†]

Beethoven and Goethe finally met in 1812. Because of the complete contrast between their natures, their relationship could not easily develop beyond the respect of one great artist for another. Goethe wrote to his close friend, the composer Carl Friedrich Zelter: "His talent amazed me; unfortunately he is an utterly untamed personality." Beethoven wrote to Breitkopf & Härtel: "Goethe is too fond of the atmosphere of the courts, more so than is becoming to a poet. Why laugh at the absurdities of virtuosi when poets, who ought to be the first teachers of a nation, forget all else for the sake of this glitter?"

Eighteen years later, Felix Mendelssohn (1809-47) wrote a letter to his sister, Fanny, which shows the continued uneasiness that Goethe felt when confronted with Beethoven's later music. Mendelssohn was twenty-one years old at the time.

    [†] From *Reisebrief . . . aus dem Jahren 1830–32*, Leipzig, 1861. Letter to his sister, Fanny, May 25, 1830, ed. G. Selden-Goth, transl. Lady Wallace, London, 1946, p. 71. Reprinted by permission of Elak Books Limited.

Goethe is so friendly and kind to me, that I don't know how to thank him sufficiently, or what to do to deserve it. Mornings I play to him for about an hour. He likes to hear the works of all the different great piano composers in chronological order and have me tell him how they have progressed. All this time he sits in a dark corner and his old eyes flash. He wanted to have nothing to do with Beethoven, but I told him I could not let him escape, and played the first part of the symphony in C minor. It had a singular effect on him; at first he said, "This arouses no emotion; nothing but astonishment; it is grandiose". He continued grumbling in this way, and after a long pause he began again, "It is very great; quite wild; it makes one fear that the house might fall down; what must it be like when all those men play together!" During dinner, in the midst of another subject, he alluded to it again. You already know that I dine with him every day; at these times he questions me very minutely, and is always so gay and communicative after dinner that we generally remain in the room by ourselves for an hour or more, while he talks on uninterruptedly.

RICHARD WAGNER[†]

In *Über das Dirigiren* (About Conducting), written in 1869, Richard Wagner (1813-83) shows both his knowledge of instrumental literature and also his practical experience as a conductor in solving problems of performance. In both the passages quoted below, Wagner implies that the instrumentalist can learn from the vocalist concerning the production of tone.

The quotation, cited above by Schenker, here reappears in context but in W. A. Ellis's translation tó conform to the rest of the passage. Where appropriate, a score reference has replaced a music example.

The best hints I ever had for the tempo and phrasing of Beethoven's music were those I once derived from the soulful, sure-accented singing of the great Schröder-Devrient[1]; it since has been impossible for me to

[†] From *Über das Dirigiren*, first published in *Neue Zeitschrift für Musik*, Nov. 26 and Dec. 17, 1869; transl. William Ashton Ellis in *Richard Wagner's Prose Works*, London, 1912, IV, 298, 311-13.

1. Wilhelmina Schröder-Devrient (1804–60), German soprano noted for the dramatic power of her operatic performances, especially in Beethoven's *Fidelio*. She created three Wagnerian roles, Adriano in *Rienzi*, Senta in *Der fliegende Holländer*, and Venus in *Tannhäuser*. [*Editor*]

allow e.g. the affecting cadenza for the oboe in the first movement of the C-minor Symphony

to be draggled in the way I have always heard elsewhere. Nay, harking back from this cadenza itself, I also found the meaning and expression for that prolonged fermata of the first violins in the corresponding passage [m. 21], and the stirring impression I won from this pair of insignificant-looking points gave me a new insight into the life of the whole movement.

* * *

To make this [i.e. the need for flexibility of tempo in creating a sensitive performance] clear by one simplest of all examples, I select the opening of the C-minor Symphony:

After quite a brief sojourn on the fermata of the second bar, our conductors pass it by, and employ that halt almost solely for concentrating the band's attention upon a sharp attack on the figure in the third bar. The E♭ is habitually held no longer than the duration of an ordinary forte taken by a careless bow. Now let us suppose the voice of Beethoven to have cried from the grave to a conductor: "Hold thou my fermata long and terribly! I wrote no fermata for jest or from bepuzzlement, haply to think out my further move; but the same full tone I mean to be squeezed dry in my Adagio for utterance of sweltering emotion, I cast among the rushing figures of my passionate Allegro, if need be, a paroxysm of joy or horror. Then shall its life be drained to the last blood-drop; then do I part the waters of my ocean, and bare the depths of its abyss; or curb the flocking herd of clouds, dispel the whirling web of mist, and open up a glimpse into the pure blue firmament, the sun's irradiate eye. For this I set fermate in my Allegros, notes entering of a sudden, and long held out. And mark thou what a definite thematic aim I had with this. sustained E♭, after a storm of three short notes, and what I meant to say by all the like held notes that follow."—Now if, upon receipt of such a warning, this conductor should suddenly ask an orchestra to give to that fermata bar the significance, and *consequently* the length he thought needful in Beethoven's sense, what result would he obtain? A most deplorable. After the 'strings' had squandered the first impact of the bow, their tone would grow the thinner the longer they were made hold on to it, and fade away in a fogged piano: for—and here I touch one of the evil issues of our modern conductors' habits,—nothing has become more foreign to our orchestras than *even strength in holding a note*. I challenge the whole body of conductors to demand a full and equably sustained forte from any instrument of the orchestra, no matter which, just to give them a taste of the surprised amazement such a claim arouses, and what patient exercise it needs to bring about the right effect.

Yet this equably sustained tone is the basis of all dynamics, as in Song, so in the Orchestra: only by making it our starting-point, can we arrive at all those modifications whose multifariousness determines the general character of execution. Without this foundation an orchestra puts forth much noise, but no power; and herein lies a first token of the feebleness of most of our orchestral doings. But, since our modern conductors know as good as nothing of it, they plume themselves instead on an *over-hushed piano*. Now, this is attainable by the 'strings' without much effort, but it costs a great deal to the 'wind,' and in particular the 'wood-wind.' From the latter, and above all the flautists—who have turned their once so gentle instruments into veritable tubes of violence,—a delicately sustained piano is hardly to be obtained any more; save perhaps from French oboists, as they never transgress the pastoral character of their instrument, or from clarinetists when one asks them for the echo effect. This evil, to be encountered in our very best orchestras, suggests the question: If the wind-players are really incapable of a smooth piano, why doesn't one try at least to maintain a balance, and make the strings replace their often positively laughable contrast by a somewhat fuller body of tone? But this disproportion plainly quite escapes the notice of our conductors. From another point of view, the fault is largely to be found in the character of the stringed instruments' piano itself: for just as we have no *true forte*, neither have we any *true piano*; both lack all roundness of tone. And here, again, our string-players might take a lesson from the 'wind'; whereas it certainly is easy enough for the former to draw the bow quite loosely across the strings, and thus produce a mere buzzing whir, it requires great artistic control of the breath to make it stream forth evenly and low, upon a wind-instrument, and yet preserve clearness and purity of intonation. Wherefore our fiddlers should learn the true round-toned piano from first-class wind-players, providing the latter have deigned to adopt it themselves from first-rate singers.

FELIX WEINGARTNER[†]

Felix Weingartner (1863-1942) was born in Dalmatia, and studied music first in Graz, then Leipzig. In 1884 started his long and illustrious career as conductor, in opera as well as concert-hall, which in some fifty years established his reputation as a "classic" interpreter of 18th and 19th century music throughout the musical world. His book on conducting is a revealing sequel to Wagner's and gives evidence about the excesses indulged in by imitators of Hans von Bülow (1830-94), Wagner's chief disciple as an interpreter.

The difficulty of getting a good *ensemble* in the tempo-rubato manner is all the greater when the conductor goes touring. Bülow for some years directed only the Meiningen orchestra, and afterwards only the Philharmonic orchestras in Hamburg and Berlin. He knew these through and through, and the players, who understood him thoroughly, followed him in every detail, so that even his caprices were rendered with faultless technique. But a conductor who comes before a strange orchestra and wants to take the works not in their natural way—wherein the feeling of the players will always assist him—but to distort them, has not the time, in the few rehearsals that are usually allowed him, to elaborate properly all these *ritenuti, accelerandi*, little *fermate*, and breath-pauses by which he hopes to make an effect; and so it may happen that some of the players follow the conductor and the others their natural feelings, and the greatest ambiguity results. It has struck me that eccentricity of this kind has been carried to further extremes in foreign tours than in our own country, apparently because the public abroad is supposed to be more easily imposed on. At least I have found in the orchestral parts abroad some markings which, had I not seen them with my own eyes, I should

† From *Über das Dirigieren*, 3rd ed., Leipzig, 1905, pp. 35–41; transl. Ernest Newman as *On Conducting*, London, 1906, pp. 34–39. A footnote has been deleted.

have thought impossible. Having often been asked by the players, before the rehearsal, whether I would adopt this or that peculiar *nuance* of one of my predecessors, I generally found it necessary to say categorically: "Ignore all markings; follow only the printed instructions as to phrasing." Since in spite of this there were misunderstandings, owing to the parts being in many places so covered with "readings" that the original was obliterated, I often protected myself later on by taking my own copies with me.

The saddest part of the business was that the chief arena chosen for all these varieties and experiments was our glorious classical music, especially the holiest of all, that of Beethoven, since Bülow had acquired the reputation of a master-conductor of Beethoven, and his followers wanted to outbid him even there; though one would have thought that reverence—to say nothing of love—for this unique genius would have put all vain thoughts of this kind to flight.

To take only one example, how the C minor Symphony has been tampered with! Already the gigantic opening has brought into being a whole crowd of readings, notably that according to which the first five bars (with the two *fermate*) are to be taken quite slowly. Even the "spirit of Beethoven" was cited to justify this misguided attempt at emendation, for which, however, not Beethoven's spirit but that of his first biographer, Schindler, is entirely responsible. Schindler, the key to whose character, I think, is sufficiently given by the fact that after the master's death he had visiting cards printed with the title "Ami de Beethoven," has told in his biography so many anecdotes whose untruth has been proved by Thayer, that we may unhesitatingly reckon among them the story that Beethoven wanted the opening of the C minor Symphony to be taken *andante*, and the faster tempo to come only after the second *fermata*. Is there even a moderately satisfactory explanation why Beethoven, instead of specifying so extremely important a change of tempo, should have marked the passage *allegro con brio* when what he wanted was *andante*? Liszt's opinion on the point will be of interest. In the previously-mentioned concert of the Meiningen orchestra in Eisenach, where I made Bülow's personal acquaintance,—he took the opening of the C minor symphony, that time at least, in a brisk *allegro*—Liszt told me that the "ignorant" and furthermore "mischievous fellow" Schindler turned up one fine day at Mendelssohn's, and tried to stuff him that Beethoven wished the opening to be *andante*—pom, pom, pom, pom. "Mendelssohn, who was usually so amiable," said Liszt laughingly, "got so enraged that he threw Schindler out—pom, pom, pom, *pom!*"

Near the end of the first movement there is at one place a five-bar group—

Now whether we look upon the fourth bar of the second group (the pause) as a short *fermata* and the first bar of the succeeding five-bar group as the up-take—according to which there then comes another four-bar sentence—or whether we take it that the opening theme of the *allegro* occurs in the recapitulation the first time thus—

and the second time with an extra bar, thus—

however we calculate the thing mathematically, in either case the short breathless silence and the ensuing outburst of the chord of the diminished seventh become, just by their prolongation, terrific, gigantic, powerful, menacing, overwhelming, volcanic. It is like a giant's fist rising from the earth. Will it be believed that almost everywhere I found the indescribable effect of this passage simply destroyed, either by a bar of the diminished-seventh chord or by the pause itself being *struck out*?

The most tasteless rhythmic distortions, the most absurd breath-pauses, have been calmly indulged in in order to appear interesting; the result has been, however, to turn a supreme stroke of genius into a mere piece of irregularity; *because* the thing must go as a four-bar phrase. *O sancta simplicitas!* The offenders always father their audacities on Bülow. I cannot believe he had so many sins to answer for.

Towards the end of the same movement, in the passage where the
chords come rattling down like devastating masses of rock,

I found the two *sforzati* corrected to an elegant *piano*, and a delicate
diminuendo marked before them, making the passage like an elegiac
sigh.

I freely admit that I have never been fully satisfied with the render-
ing of the second movement of this symphony under any conductor but
Bülow. Beethoven marks it *andante con moto*. The older conductors
overlooked the "con moto" and played the movement *andante*; the
modern ones, on the other hand, appear to see only the "con moto," and
drop into an *allegretto*, thus giving the wonderful theme

a dance-like character that is quite alien to its nature. My own conception of it, in which the *andante* is maintained while the *con moto* is
regarded as the spiritual breath that unites and animates the movement,
I cannot adequately express in words; I must refer to the performances I
am permitted to give of the work.

I may mention a tragi-comic incident I once witnessed in this movement. After the conductor had begun in the usual *allegretto*, he played
these bars—

in so slow a tempo that he had to beat each semiquaver of the triplet sep-
arately! But enough of these examples.

I need mention no names in order to point out that several conductors of importance have refused to have anything to do with these perversions of style. I may also say that my remarks refer for the most part to an epoch now somewhat removed from ours. When I published this book in 1895, my object was to try to show how much the art of conducting had developed up to then, since the time when Wagner had given it a new basis both by his deeds and his words. If on the one hand a decided progress could be noted,—greater competence in the orchestra, a more perfect *ensemble,* more feeling for vital phrasing than hitherto, thanks to Bülow and some excellent conductors who had become great under Wagner's direct influence,—on the other hand there was imminent danger that the vanity, egoism and caprice of younger conductors should make fashionable a style in which the masterpieces of music should be merely pegs on which to hang a conductor's own personal caprices. This is all the more dangerous as an audience with little artistic education may, in its astonishment, take the arbitrary for the genuine thing, and, its healthy feeling once perverted, always hanker after these unsound piquancies, so that finally it thinks the trickiest performance the best. Wagner's treatise combated the philistinism that suffocated every modification of tempo and therefore all vitality of phrasing in a rigid metronomism; my own book on the other hand combated the errors that had arisen through exaggeration of these modifications after the necessity for them had gradually come to be admitted. It was therefore no plagiarism of Wagner's, as was of course asserted, but its counterpart, or, if you will, its continuation in the spirit of our own day. If Wagner opened new paths, I believed it my duty to warn people against mistaking a senseless trampling of the grass for progress along new paths.

DONALD FRANCIS TOVEY [†]

When musicians regard the last forty-odd bars of Beethoven's C minor Symphony as a meaningless noise they are as far from the truth as

[†] From Donald Francis Tovey, *A Musician Talks*, Volume II: *Musical Textures,* London, 1941, p. 64. Published by Oxford University Press; reprinted by permission.

the most naïve listener to whom a fugue is a tuneless chaos. These forty bars are meaningless without the rest of the symphony, but the symphony ends as truly within its own length as the *Et in terra pax* of the B-minor Mass.

EDWARD T. CONE[†]

Edward T. Cone (b. 1917) is a composer, writer, and teacher, for over twenty years a member of the music department at Princeton University.

Composers as a rule open a score either with the first attack, or with the minimum number of rests essential for easy reading; but they often end with indications of extra time—by *fermatas* or even blank measures. But where this is not done, the implication of silent measures is still often inescapable. The score of Beethoven's Fifth Symphony begins with an eighth rest, but surely this is a device to prevent misreading of the triple upbeat that follows. No one can hear it as a silent downbeat. At the end of the movement, however, the four-measure pattern has been so firmly established that one is forced to add a silent measure after the last one notated—a measure that is as essentially a part of the composition as those actually written.

In general, there is no such thing as true redundancy in music. In the case of a reiterated motif, for instance, we cannot say, "Now we get the point, so let's have something different." The point lies precisely in the fact that we get nothing different, but rather another repetition, and another, and still another, and yet another. (To take an example from a verbal medium, compare the cumulative effect of King Lear's "Never, never, never, never, never!") It is true, of course, that there are psychological and esthetic limits to the amount of repetition allowable. What is at first effective soon becomes comical and eventually boring. (Try adding a few more "nevers" to Lear's line.) It is only at this point that we can speak of redundancy—when each additional statement adds noth-

† From *Musical Form and Musical Performance*, New York, 1968, pp. 18, 46–47. Copyright © 1968 by W. W. Norton & Co., Inc.

ing new. Here, of course, we are once again facing Satie's wallpaper—and some of Warhol's movies.

From the performer's point of view, the practical problem arises when he is faced with the decision whether or not to make a repeat that seems purely conventional. But how often are such repeats purely conventional? Why, for example, was Beethoven so insistent that the exposition of the *Eroica* should be repeated? In this and similar instances, one can often adduce a number of reasons, any one of which would be sufficient to explain such a stance.

In the first place, in the case of a new work, a repetition of the exposition gives the audience another opportunity of absorbing its material. Such a consideration is no longer valid for Beethoven symphonies, but it might well have proved crucial for the comprehension of their early performances.

Much more important today is the question of proportions. Look at the first movement of Beethoven's Fifth Symphony. It is so short that there can be no excuse for suppressing the repeat; yet this is often done—with adverse effect. Its four sections—exposition, development, recapitulation, and coda—are so nearly the same length that the focus of the movement is blurred by the simple alternation of equal parts: statement–development–statement–development (for the coda is, of course, a second development). The repetition of the exposition effects the needed balance by strengthening the expository sections: AABAC.

A point that often seems insignificant, but is by no means always so, concerns the frequent appearance of a transitional return as a first ending. Even the few measures in this position in the *Eroica* are too good to miss. How much more important is the first ending of Mendelssohn's *Italian* Symphony. Here the composer introduces a new theme, one to which he will not again advert until the coda. Suppression of the first ending ruins the intended formal effect.

Bibliography

BEETHOVEN'S LIFE, WORK, LETTERS

Anderson, Emily, ed. and transl., *Letters of Beethoven*, 3 vols., New York, 1961. A small selection from this work has been edited by Alan Tyson: *Selected Letters of Beethoven*, New York, 1967. This version is available in paperback.

Burk, John N., *The Life and Works of Beethoven*, New York, 1943. Perhaps the most reliable short biography in English.

Kinsky, Georg, *Das Werk Beethovens*, completed and edited by Hans Halm, Munich, 1955. This is the complete and definitive thematic catalogue of Beethoven's compositions.

Reizler, Walter, *Beethoven*, transl. G. D. H. Pidcock, New York, 1938. A thoughtful discussion of Beethoven's music.

Sonneck, Oscar, ed. and transl., *Beethoven: Impressions of Contemporaries*, New York, 1926. Available in a Dover paperback as *Beethoven: Impressions by His Contemporaries*.

Thayer's Life of Beethoven, 2nd ed., rev. and ed. Elliot Forbes, 2 vols., Princeton, N.J., 1967. Available in paperback, 1 vol. Alexander Wheelock Thayer's work in Beethoven biography is basic. The work first appeared in German in five volumes with the help of Herman Deiters and Hugo Riemann. The first edition of Vol. 1 was published in 1866; in 1908 the final volume was published by Riemann after the deaths of both Thayer and Deiter. The first edition in English was published by Henry Edward Krehbiel in three volumes in 1921.

THE SYMPHONIES

Berlioz, Hector, *Etude critique des symphonies de Beethoven*, in *A travers chants*, 2nd ed., Paris, 1872, pp. 17-62. This study has been translated by Edwin Evans: *A Critical Study of Beethoven's Nine Symphonies*, London, 1913 (reprinted in 1958).

Evans, Edwin, *Beethoven's Nine Symphonies*, New York, 1923. A full description and superficial analysis.

Grove, George, *Beethoven and his Nine Symphonies*, London, 1896. There is a 1962 Dover paperback of the 3rd ed. (1898). Sir George Grove was the first Englishman to analyse the symphonies in depth. He was in communication with Thayer. Both men approached the music with the love of the amateur.

Nef, Karl, *Die neun Sinfonien Beethovens*, Leipzig, 1928. This book is rich in references to the writings on the symphonic literature up to that time.

Prod'homme, Jacques-Gabriel, *Les symphonies de Beethoven*, Paris, 1906. New and rev. ed., 1949. The most comprehensive work by a French musician.

SPECIAL STUDIES IN ENGLISH

Carse, Adam, *The Sources of Beethoven's Fifth Symphony*, in *Music and Letters*, XXIX (1948), 249-62.

Chusid, Martin, *Schubert's Cyclic Compositions of 1824*, in *Acta Musicologica*, XXXVI/1 (1964), 40-45.

Gregory, Robin, *The Horn in Beethoven's Symphonies*, in *Music and Letters*, XXXIII/4 (1952), 303-10.

Hirsch, Paul, *A Discrepancy in Beethoven*, in *Music and Letters*, XIX (1938), 265-67.

La Rue, Jan, *Harmonic Rhythm in the Beethoven Symphonies*, in *Music Review*, VXIII/1 (1957), 8-20.

Simpson, Robert, *The First Version of Beethoven's C minor Symphony*, in *The Score*, No. 26 (1960), 30-34.

Tyson, Alan, *Sketches and Autographs*, in *The Beethoven Companion*, London, 1971, pp. 443-89. Particularly p. 455.

Tyson, Alan, *Notes on Five of Beethoven's Copyists*, in *Journal of the American Musicological Society*, XXIII/3 (Fall 1970), 439-71.

Weingartner, Felix, *On the Performance of Beethoven's Symphonies*, transl. Jessie Crosland (1907), reprinted in paperback in *Weingartner On Music and Conducting*, New York, 1969.

SPECIAL STUDIES IN GERMAN

Göhler, Georg, *Die Führung der melodischen Linie in Beethovens C-Moll-Sinfonie*, in *Zeitschrift für Musik*, XCI/2 (1924), 60-66.

Müller-Reuter, Theodor, *Bilder und Klänge des Friedens*, Leipzig, 1919. See Chapter 4, "Die rhythmische Bedeutung der Hauptmotivs im ersten Satze der fünften Sinfonie."